MW01681591

Invoking the Holy Spirit

A Guide to Awakening

In Your True Self, Your True Home, The Holy Spirit.

By

Moustapha Kemal Ozturk

Table of Content

DEDICATION I
ACKNOWLEDGEMENTS II
ABOUT THE AUTHOR III
AUTHOR'S PREFACE IV
INTRODUCTION 1
CHAPTER 1 YOUR ALWAYS CREATING 3
CHAPTER 2 AWARENESS THE INVISIBLE BEING YOU ARE.........................5
CHAPTER 3 WE ARE ALL GODS CHILDREN..8
CHAPTER 4 YOU ARE A PRISONER OF THE 'MAYA' - THE GREAT PLAY OF LIFE 9
CHAPTER 5 RETURN TO OUR FATHER 11
CHAPTER 6 EVERYTHING PERCEIVED CAN BE SEEN IN EITHER OF TWO WAYS 14
CHAPTER 7 WE DON'T NEED NO BODY! 17
CHAPTER 8 UNFORGIVENESS, THE CROSS WE CARRY 19
CHAPTER 9 SAVE YOUR SELF WITH YOUR UNCONDITIONAL LOVE 22
CHAPTER 10 WE CREATE THE GIFTS WE GIVE TO OURSELVES 24
CHAPTER 11 EVERYTHING PERCEIVED IS ILLUSION EXCEPT FORGIVENESS 27
CHAPTER 12 WE ARE NO THING!...29
CHAPTER 13 PEACE IS OUR JOURNEYS END...31
CHAPTER 14 GOD IS IN ALL OF US 33
CHAPTER 15 CHRIST GODS LOVE IS UNCONDITIONAL 35
CHAPTER 16 SALVATION'S ONLY OBSTACLE IS ME 37
CHAPTER 17 WE ARE NOT BOUND BY EARTHLY LAWS 40
CHAPTER 18 CREATING A SPACE FOR INSERTING GODS DIVINE THOUGHT 42
CHAPTER 19 YOU ARE THE PROJECTOR NOT THE SCREEN 45
CHAPTER 20 WE CONDEMN OURSELVES..47
CHAPTER 21 WE ARE FORMLESS 48
CHAPTER 22 WE ARE MIND WITH FREE WILL 50
CHAPTER 23 CREATED IN GODS MIND 51
CHAPTER 24 THE EGO STEPS ASIDE 52
CHAPTER 25 EVERYTHING MISTAKEN THOUGHTS.................................53
CHAPTER 26 MAGIC DUST..55
CHAPTER 27 LOVE IS NATURAL 57
CHAPTER 28 LOVE IS WHAT I AM 61
CHAPTER 29 MY THOUGHTS ARE NOT MY OWN 63
CHAPTER 30 WE ARE NOT IN OUR RIGHT MINDS 66
CHAPTER 31 UNFORGIVEN THOUGHTS BLIND US TO LOVE 68

CHAPTER 32 LOVING PEACE....69
CHAPTER 33 REMEMBER GOD....71
CHAPTER 34 PUT YOUR FAITH IN GODS THOUGHTS....73
CHAPTER 35 EVER HAD A PET?....75
CHAPTER 36 EARTHLY THOUGHTS ARE DESIGNED TO KEEP US FEARFUL.77
CHAPTER 37 LIVING IN SIN IS LIVING AS EMBRYONIC MANKIND....79
CHAPTER 38 TRUST IN FORGIVENESS....80
CHAPTER 39 WHEN IN DOUBT....81
CHAPTER 40 SURRENDER TO CHRIST GOD....82
CHAPTER 41 AWAKENING TO GOD'S LOVE....84
CHAPTER 42 HAVE NO EXPECTATIONS....85
CHAPTER 43 REFRAIN FROM JUDGING....86
CHAPTER 44 ACCEPT ONLY GOD'S LOVING THOUGHTS....87
CHAPTER 45 THERE IS ONLY ONE LIVING CONSCIOUSNESS....88
CHAPTER 46 BE LOVE FIRST ABOVE ANYTHING....90
CHAPTER 47 YOU, ME, FATHER, BROTHER....92
CHAPTER 48 UNPLUG YOURSELF....94
CHAPTER 49 DON'T HIDE FROM YOUR LIFE....95
CHAPTER 50 REST IN NON-JUDGEMENT....96
CHAPTER 51 EVERYTHING IS ILLUSION....98
CHAPTER 52 THE ILLUSION CAN GIVE YOU NOTHING....100
CHAPTER 53 IGNORE EARTHLY FLACK....101
CHAPTER 54 EVICT THE STRANGER....103
CHAPTER 55 FOR-GIVE-IT-ALL-AWAY....105
CHAPTER 56 IT IS GODS WILL WE KNOW OF GOOD AND EVIL THEN COME HOME....106
CHAPTER 57 GUARD YOUR MIND....108
CHAPTER 58 GOD IS OUR ONLY TRUE HOME....110
CHAPTER 59 BRING TO THE FORE YOUR TRUE SELF....111
CHAPTER 60 WE HAVE REPLACED LOVE WITH FEAR.....112
CHAPTER 61 LET GO OF TIRESOME IDOLS....114
CHAPTER 62 PUT THE LID BACK ON PANDORA'S BOX....115
CHAPTER 63 WHOLENESS....117
CHAPTER 64 LOVE ONLY CREATES....118
CHAPTER 65 SINFUL THOUGHTS....119
CHAPTER 66 FATHER LIKE SON....121
CHAPTER 67 FORGIVENESS A COSMIC ANTI-GRAVITY FORCE....123
CHAPTER 68 LOOPING THOUGHTS....125
CHAPTER 69 OWN YOUR MULTIVERSE....127
CHAPTER 70 ANOTHER WAY OF LIVING....129
CHAPTER 71 CHRIST OUR TRUE FACE....131
CHAPTER 72 CHRIST VISION....132

CHAPTER 73 STOP HIDING YOUR SELF BEHIND TEMPTATIONS............133
CHAPTER 74 BE YOUR OWN WATCHMAN 136
CHAPTER 75 HIS VISION REPLACES HUMAN SIGHT..............................138
CHAPTER 76 YOUR MIND IS YOUR SANCTUARY - GUARD IT 140
CHAPTER 77 KNOW TRUTH WITH CHRIST VISION...................................142
CHAPTER 78 GRAFTED TO GHOSTS..144
CHAPTER 79 THE GOLDEN NUGGET..146
CHAPTER 80 MAKING ROOM FOR OUR CREATORS CREATIVE THOUGHTS
....148
CHAPTER 81 REST IN GODS SILENT THOUGHTS 150
CHAPTER 82 THE SCULPTOR THINKS HE'S THE STATUE HE MADE.........151
CHAPTER 83 LIVING WITHOUT ANXIETY..153
CHAPTER 84 LET GO OF CONTROL..155
CHAPTER 85 IN THEIR ORIGINAL WRAPPING......................................157
CHAPTER 86 MISSING YOUR TRAIN STOP..158
CHAPTER 87 REMEMBER YOUR ONLY ACTING 160
CHAPTER 88 I'M STILL SNARED 162
CHAPTER 89 TWO WAYS TO SEE 164
CHAPTER 90 YOUR MIND A BATTLE GROUND 166
CHAPTER 91 THE RED CARPET..167
CHAPTER 92 YOUR MIND ALL TIED UP 169
CHAPTER 93 LOSE ONE WORLD...171
CHAPTER 94 THE GAME IS UP 173
CHAPTER 95 GIFT YOUR NEUTRAL BEING TO CHRIST...........................175
CHAPTER 96 SILENT MIND..177
CHAPTER 97 TRUE PERFECT SELF..179
CHAPTER 98 REST IN NEUTRALITY..180
CHAPTER 99 EXTINGUISH THE FIRE 182
CHAPTER 100 CHRISTS SECOND COMING...184
CHAPTER 101 INSTANT SALVATION..185
CHAPTER 102 EASIER SAID THAN DONE 187
CHAPTER 103 SWITCHING CHANNELS 188
CHAPTER 104 THE DRAW BRIDGE 190
CHAPTER 105 WE CANNOT BE TWO..192
CHAPTER 106 EVERYTHING OUTSIDE OF YOU IS NOTHING...................195
CHAPTER 107 A LOT MORE FUN...197
CHAPTER 108 WAKE UP TO GODS WILL...198
CHAPTER 109 YOUR POWER IS NOW SEIZE IT 200
CHAPTER 110 UNTARNISHED BY SIN 202
CHAPTER 111 ALL GOD'S CHILDREN 203
CHAPTER 112 CHERISH THE HOLY SON..204
CHAPTER 113 WE REMAIN CONNECTED TO THE VINE 205

CHAPTER 114 OPEN YOUR HEART AND FEEL HIS PEACE AND LOVE SURROUNDING YOU 207
CHAPTER 115 LET HIM FILL YOU 208
CHAPTER 116 OUR ATONEMENT 210
CHAPTER 117 HUMBLE YOURSELF 211
CHAPTER 118 YOUR NEVER ALONE 212
CHAPTER 119 FEAR POWER OR GODS LOVE POWER, YOU CHOOSE 213
CHAPTER 120 THE PUPPET 215
CHAPTER 121 THE ORIGINAL FEAR 218
CHAPTER 122 THE MIRACLES MAKING - BE CAREFUL WHAT YOU WISH FOR 221
CHAPTER 123 HE IS MY BROTHER 228
CHAPTER 124 BE PATIENT 229
CHAPTER 125 LOSING OUR FOCUS 230
CHAPTER 126 GHOSTLY THOUGHTS 232
CHAPTER 127 THE PICKPOCKET 233
CHAPTER 128 BE THE HAPPIEST CHILD IN THE ROOM 236
CHAPTER 129 ATONE AND LET YOUR SINLESSNESS BE KNOW 238
CHAPTER 130 PULL OUT THE WEEDS 240
CHAPTER 131 TRANSMUTE YOUR ANXIETIES WITH COURAGE INTO LOVE 242
CHAPTER 132 ONE SOUL IS ALL IT TAKES 244
CHAPTER 133 LOVE IS ALL WE CAN CARRY 245
CHAPTER 134 YOUR HOLY SANCTUARY AWAITS YOU UNDEFILED 246
CHAPTER 135 TAP THE SOURCE OF LOVE ITSELF 248
CHAPTER 136 RESTORED TO UNITY 253
CHAPTER 137 THE FAKE WILL 255
CHAPTER 138 GIFT YOUR BODY TO CHRIST 257
CHAPTER 139 SHAKE IT OFF 260
CHAPTER 140 REMEMBER GODS LOVE 262
CHAPTER 141 LOVE ATTRACTS ITSELF 264
CHAPTER 142 NOTHING TO DO 267
CHAPTER 143 YOUR HIDDEN TORCH 269
CHAPTER 144 REBORN INTO CHRIST HOOD 272
CHAPTER 145 TAKE REFUGE UNDER BLUE SKIES 273
CHAPTER 146 VCR GOGGLES AND HEADPHONES 278
CHAPTER 147 CALL UPON YOUR TRUE SELF 280
CHAPTER 148 THE ELEPHANT IN THE ROOM 283
CHAPTER 149 MYSELF IN CHRIST GOD IS EVERYTHING 285
CHAPTER 150 LAUGH AT JUDGEMENT 288
CHAPTER 151 TAMING THE RAYS 289
CHAPTER 152 WARP SPEED AHEAD 291
CHAPTER 153 THE OCTOPUS AND THE DRAIN PIPE 293

CHAPTER 154 THE SPINNING ELECTRON 295
CHAPTER 155 SEEING HOLINESS ALL AROUND 300
CHAPTER 156 THE SCRAM ENGINE 303
CHAPTER 157 YOUR MIND THE GATEWAY TO GOD 307
CHAPTER 158 UNCLOG YOUR MIND 309
CHAPTER 159 CREATED IN HIS LIKENESS 310
CHAPTER 160 HEAL YOURSELF 311
CHAPTER 161 LIVING IN BRILLIANCE 313
CHAPTER 162 HEARING GODS VOICE 315
CHAPTER 163 YOUR JUDGEMENTS ARE YOUR PRISON WALLS 317
CHAPTER 164 DWELL IN GODS THOUGHTS 319
CHAPTER 165 GODS PARADIGM 321
CHAPTER 166 FORGIVING SIGHT 323
CHAPTER 167 THE BEST SEAT IN THE HOUSE 325
CHAPTER 168 EVERYTHING IS MAGIC 327
CHAPTER 169 BRING THE BILL 329
CHAPTER 170 THE CHRYSALIS 332
CHAPTER 171 THE LIVING PRESENCE 335
CHAPTER 172 HUNGER FOR GODS THOUGHTS 337
AUTHORS GLOSSARY / MEANING OF TERMS 341

Dedication

I dedicate this book to all those who seek their truth in our Lord God, who have gone before and will go after, for eternity.

Acknowledgements

I am deeply thankful to Stonebridge Publishers and the team, including Jill and Anne. My gratitude goes to my family and friends, especially Lisa, whose encouragement led me to write this book and see it through to publication.

About the Author

Moustapha Kemal Ozturk was born in Cyprus and moved to England between the ages of one and two years old. After graduating from the University of Surrey, he began working in the UK construction industry. At the age of 28, in the spring of 1988, he experienced remarkable events that led him to embark on what would become a 37-year journey of self-discovery and spiritual development.

Author's Preface

I guess my spiritual journey really started at the turn of winter's end and the early spring of 1988. In the months preceding the events, I would say my life was in turmoil. Left with a broken heart after a failed five-year relationship at twenty-eight years old, I drifted for months from job to job, relationship to relationship, with no definite plan.

Then, one night in early March 1988, I remember screaming to myself in my head the words, "God, help me understand." Feeling exhausted after what had become a pattern of long working hours and late nights out, I fell asleep.

At the time, I was working as a construction manager at a building site in South London. Shortly after my desperate plea for understanding the next day almost, I think the strange telephone calls started, received in my work site office. Back then, no one had easy-carry mobile phones like we do today, because they weren't invented. The fixed landline was the norm. A Motorola-type mobile phone was available, but you had to carry it with a battery the size of a suitcase. The callers, however, preferred the fixed landlines.

Typically, the callers would ask, "Where's Moustapha? Tell him to come home, his dinner is ready." Or they would say, "Tell Moustapha I'm coming to the site with a six-week-old baby," or, "a six-day-old baby," in the middle of the night, frightening the security guard on duty, who threatened to call the police.

In the daytime, once I picked up the phone and heard the voices of what I can only describe as multitudes on the other end laughing, which gave me chills. This went on for a whole month strange phone calls. One particular call sticks out in my memory: the caller told the guard, "Tell Moustapha to come home, the baby has swallowed a marble." It would not be until this year that I realised the significance of the marbles, after watching a scene in the movie where Oppenheimer would have regular updates from the US Defence Department on the production of enriched plutonium and uranium. They would put marbles into two goldfish bowls. When the marbles reached the top of the bowl, they had enough for one atom bomb.

Anyway, going back to early 1988 and my life, in the weeks before these strange calls I was searching for answers. I was fleetingly reading the Bible a girlfriend at the time had bought for me. I also remember reading parts of the Koran. I had a good understanding of evolution at this time too. Unknown to me, 'the idea' was beginning to take shape in my head an idea that would develop into a complete answer to all the big questions I had asked God to help me understand.

Then one night, after a girlfriend decided she didn't want to see me anymore because I had told her the night before that I was going to Spain to live for a few months, she refused to answer the front door to me.

So, I left her doorstep and started to head back, in the early hours shortly after midnight, to my apartment in Finchley, North London. It was early April by then a two-hour drive right across central London. I was about twenty minutes away from my home, driving through the Swiss Cottage area, when the penny suddenly dropped in my mind. I remembered a quote from Genesis: "Let us make man in our own image." Us. In our. Our image.

I realised at that moment that the world I thought I was living in was not original; it was a replica a replica of an ancient world that had long since died but, somehow, the memories of its existence had been perfectly preserved for you, for me, and for billions and zillions of future generations of God's children to know of their ancestry.

I decided to turn the car around. Realising it was getting so late, I thought I might as well drive to work, as I needed to be there in four or five hours anyway, and I could catch some sleep in my car.

I had never turned up like that before, in the middle of the night, to any of the construction sites I had previously worked on. I walked into the site office, and the guard looked at me in almost shock. Just a few minutes earlier, he had put down the phone to a woman who had said, "Moustapha is heading to the site. Please tell him to come home."

I think that was the last call. After that, nothing other than the guard later reporting to me that three people had visited the site on a Sunday, when it was closed, looking for me.

In the intervening 37 years since the calls, I have been blessed with good health, developing my ideas further whilst remaining in construction. I eventually settled down, raised a family, and that family grew and grew, eventually into grandchildren.

I retired at the end of June this year and decided to finish this book, which I had been writing inadvertently over the last couple of years.

Just a brief context on how the book came to be. My book is a collection of my notes made whilst studying *The Course in Miracles*, which I began reading for the second time in 2023 and continued until June of this year. Mostly, I would study the book and make my notes during my early morning train journeys to work, which typically lasted a little over two hours.

Very soon after starting the course, I noticed that during many of these study sessions, as I was typing my notes as text messages to myself, I would seamlessly drift into a deep sense of peace. It felt as if my hand, tapping away on my phone screen, was no longer my own, and that my mind and body were being used by a determined somebody inside me. After a while, I accepted that this is what is meant by being filled with the Holy Spirit.

I deliberately haven't quoted from *The Course in Miracles* because I want my book to stand on its own, and also for the reader not to be distracted if they are familiar with the course. I would write my notes, that is, each chapter in my book, as I studied typically one chapter a day of the course.

Anyway, that's how I arrived at the substance of the book, and when I retired in June this year, 2025, I immediately set my goal to complete it as quickly as possible.

Introduction

Many years ago, before I understood the purpose of the Holy Spirit, I was working as a building site manager on a construction site called "Villiers House", next door to Charing Cross Station in central London.

Around lunchtime on a hot summer's day, the hoist driver alerted me to a fire on the roof. I quickly made my way to the roof of this multi storey office building with my colleague, having grabbed some fire extinguishers on the way. At this stage, the fire had spread from the asphalt machine, which was the cause, to three five foot tall gas bottles that had horizontal jets of flame shooting out from them.

After emptying the fire extinguishers, which had no effect, I remember turning to my colleague, hearing the fire engines approaching, and saying that we should leave this to the fire brigade. My colleague stepped back from the fire and I chose to go in the opposite direction to retrieve my two way radio so I could alert the rest of the site management to the situation.

Having recovered my radio, I took a different route that led me past several empty five foot tall gas bottles. Suddenly, a voice sounded in my head, loud and clear, saying "Hit the deck." Instantly, I did exactly that. I threw myself to the floor just as the first gas bottle exploded. The fireball swept directly over me, but I was shielded by the row of empty gas bottles. I picked myself up and ran towards my colleague, gaining some distance before the second and third gas bottles exploded. We both escaped uninjured.

It was years later before I realised that the Holy Spirit lives within all of us, not outside us, and that on that hot summer's day He saved my life.

The purpose of this book is to guide its readers to trust and call upon the Holy Spirit daily, for He lives at the centre of their beingness, their true self. In doing so, they can ensure the best outcomes for their lives.

Chapter 1
Your always Creating

You are always creating. Everything and everyone can be perceived as a gift you create and give to yourself. God's unconditional love is always ready and waiting for your acceptance, to enhance your gifts and to co-create with shared thoughts the apprentice and the master craftsman working together, shaping and creating our world.

Always remember, God our Creator has never left us. It is our false image of ourselves, our egos, which overlays His and our unconditional love through unforgiveness, judgements, mistrust, closed-mindedness, non-acceptance, and defensiveness everything borne of fear, which we find in our creation, our multiverse, and our perceptions to be frightening and unacceptable.

To feel your unconditional love, you must continually give it.

As you give your love to your multiverse, and to everyone and everything you perceive within it, you give it to yourself. Your goal must be to continually give your love to everyone and everything you perceive, unconditionally and without prejudice. You achieve this by repelling anxieties, judgements, and thoughts that would otherwise make you fear and reject your love. Love and hate cannot coexist in your being at the same moment. It is one or the other love or hate.

Your faith increases and is magnified as your love, God's love, and shared love flow as one upon everything you perceive. So be one in God, taking from your and His infinite store of love. As you do, do not judge His or your gifts that you give to yourself. It is your judgements that turn God's and your perfect gifts into the lesser version that you witness our fearful world.

Ideas can guide you to it, but it can only be understood experientially, by giving your love unconditionally to everything in your multiverse everything in your life.

Chapter 2

Awareness the invisible Being You are

Awareness is the invisible beingness of what we are. It is permanent and indestructible. Often called the light, with faith and courage it burns brighter, stepping forward into the present moment and dislodging the impostor who would usurp it.

Everything we have witnessed so far on Earth, the knowledge of good and evil of embryonic Earth and embryonic mankind, has either dimmed or increased our light.

Our light increases with forgiveness and non-judgement of the embryonic Earth and mankind, and decreases with hate and judgement of the embryonic Earth and embryonic mankind.

So, do not judge, and forgive away the pain experienced in the world of good and evil in your perception.

Our faith burns brighter as we worry less, judge less, and forgive more as we witness the embryonic Earth. Your goal is to not worry or fear at all as you perceive the embryonic Earth and mankind, having forgiven everything with your unconditional forgiveness, seeing through and beyond to witness heavenly bliss, with Christ

Vision cloaked with your Holy Spirit, as you merge back into what you are, Oneness with God, our Creator.

It is not your earthly body that gives you true vision and true sight. Human language is limited, and everything bodily is illusionary and can be seen in truth only when seen correctly, through forgiveness and non-judgement.

It is your faith that lights up what you look upon, blessing and transforming Earth into Heaven, your light continually blessing your multiverse.

So, increase your faith by not worrying and by forgiving away every earthly doubting thought, and by not judging. Make it your goal to see in Christ God Vision, revealing Heaven where it always was, waiting for your return from your dream of the embryonic Earth.

Your blessings light up your world. Your faith gives birth to Christ Vision, seeing the world in total forgiveness. Your acceptance, trust, and freedom from defensiveness increase your blessings, as God adds to them more, making your world more heavenly and more blissful.

When you have grasped the truth that you are this real and miraculous being of light, and that it burns brighter because of your understanding of the mechanism of how it works, to trust, to forgive, to accept, to remain open-minded and without defensiveness, when you have grasped this, understood it fully, and practise it continually each moment of your life, then your light just keeps getting brighter and brighter. It reaches a point where it cannot be contained, as God adds to your light further and further, as you worry less, judge less, and forgive more.

If you do not already, practise meditation. Find a quiet spot, close your eyes, let go of your worries and worldly attachments, and allow your mind to be filled with God's silent thoughts. Meditation experientially demonstrates how important it is to let go of the illusionary world and to find true vision in a mind at peace, cleansed of earthly worries and thoughts.

You have the power to mould your multiverse to be exactly as you want it, and God is always there, ready to make it heavenly by adding His light to your creativity.

Chapter 3

We are all Gods Children

We are all God's children, and all the pain and suffering we witness daily is our illusionary creation of the embryonic Earth, the home of our cosmic ancestors.

The ending of our torment in their suffering, and the truth of who we are in God's truth, can, in an instant, be known if only we could end the never-ending stream of earthly thoughts that sweep our minds away. That moment will only come when, at last, He, the Son of God, continually forgives away all pain and all judgement.

Free from judgement and pain, His remembrance of His Father is finally known, upon which His, and the salvation of the entire world, is given.

Chapter 4

You are a prisoner of the 'Maya' - the great play of life

We are all God's children and have allowed what we create and perceive to imprison ourselves by believing that is what we are. Instead of remembering to remain detached through continual forgiveness, we have allowed judgement and fear, partnering with temptation, to imprison ourselves and each other in the "Maya," the light show, the play of the embryonic earth.

Be aware of what has caused your imperfect vision and know you are not what you perceive. Remember, you are awareness itself, the background, the observer, and the creator of an illusion in which your awareness has been snared by your non-acceptance, judgements, unforgiveness, and temptations, the consequence of not standing guard over your mind.

The solution is simply to guard your mind, to remember and believe you are a Holy Child of God, whereupon your perceptions can be replaced forever with true vision, that of a perfect Heaven, seen in Christ's vision.

If you believed only a fraction of the truth of what you really are, you would be raised to God's Heavenly presence immediately, upon which your salvation and that of your world would finally be completed.

Remember, the Child of God exists in all of us and requires only one of us to awaken through total understanding to set himself and his brothers free. Until that moment, through our doubts, we imprison each other in the ancient world of our cosmic ancestors.

Chapter 5
Return to our Father

Greater than ever, as the great play of life of our ancient embryonic ancestors comes to an end, God our Father wants us to return Home and to remember His Love. For that to happen, we need to continually forgive everything we perceive away, everything we have created with the earthly thoughts we have accepted. We cannot be anxious, judge, hate, or hold onto any earthly emotion that binds us to their primitive world.

Through detachment from everything perceived, the door to salvation will open automatically. Perfectly formed by God's Love and cloaked in His Holy Spirit, our graduation robe, we will enter His and our Heavenly Home in Oneness.

Heaven is formless, existing in God's Mind. In God's thoughts we exist as His children, each of us with our own wills, independent extensions of His Mind. Fear cannot create, and we cannot create while our minds are fixated on the illusory earthly forms we think are real. Forgiveness is the only way to detach our minds from earthly emotions, judgements, hatred, anger, everything opposite to love, and all borne of fear. Forgiveness is the key to unlocking our attachments to the earth and our way home to love and our true creative potential.

His children who see continually and unconditionally through the lens of forgiveness and non-judgement do so from their home in Heaven, the formless source of all creation. With their creative potential and Christ Vision, they see Heaven and earth as one, perfectly at peace within itself, and all of God's children free brothers and sisters all at home.

A forgiven, quiet mind unlocks Christ Vision by cleansing our thoughts so that we look upon a perfect earth, the treasure trove of creation, with God's thoughts to guide us. The consequence of vision without forgiveness is a barren, desolate world. Expect the least from a position of formlessness and view your world through the lens of forgiveness, whereupon your thoughts are cleansed and Christ Vision of our world reveals perfect gifts in everything, everywhere, and everyone you think and create with God.

Each day, see everyone and everything as a gift, an opportunity not to judge, to accept, to forgive away any anxiety and pain, and an opportunity to bless. Every opportunity seized and mastered is another step closer to salvation, another opportunity to save yourself and your brother.

Deny each other love, and you deny God's love for you, His child. Gift love to each other so we can receive love from God. Remember to give your love freely, unconditionally, and without prejudice, as you receive it from Love's Source in perfect purity, as it is received, without contaminating it with anxieties, pains, and doubts.

Our minds can easily be fixated on illusory earthly forms we think are real. That is why nothing really changes, as we are stuck in the same patterns, the same human behaviours. Forgiveness is the only way to detach our minds from earthly emotions, judgements, hatred, anger, everything opposite to love, and all borne of fear. It is the way home.

Chapter 6
Everything perceived can be seen in either of two ways

Only with God's Will can we, His children, escape the knowing of good and evil of the imperfect earth.

God exists always in our being, even when we think we are alone and lost in this world. Through this joining of His and our being lies the means to break out from our earthly imprisonment, which we have seemingly created with our worrisome thoughts hijacking our minds and awareness.

Everything perceived can be seen in either of two ways: through the lens of hate or through the lens of love.

Forgiveness is an all-encompassing cure for all your suffering and that of the whole world, and once mastered in all experiences, your salvation and that of the world is complete.

When you are tempted, remember to continually invoke forgiveness. Let it be your shield, keeping you and everyone in heavenly peace.

Before temptation, and for all experiences, be ready always, like a sentry guard, to forgive away any intrusive earthly thoughts that would make you worry and suffer.

Remember, we are mind and not the illusionary body. If we experience pain or discomfort in any situation, then there is a lesson to be learnt: our forgiveness is required to move on.

We, God's children, through simple thoughts of forgiveness, can feel His love and remember Him.

God's Son's salvation is guaranteed, and his peace and rest remain undisturbed eternally after he has conquered forgiveness in all experiences and the earth has run its course.

Thoughts of time and worries of past and future impede your progress and prevent your mind from focusing on the present. Out of integrity, focus purely on forgiveness and non-judgement. Forgive away any anxieties and pain distracting your awareness from the present moment, and rapidly cut through remaining obstacles. Forgive away the worrying thoughts that resurface in your mind and prevent your presence from entering the foreground, the present moment, creating space for God's Shared Thoughts to bless your life.

Expediting your awakening through meditation allows you to bring to the surface of your mind all buried pain hidden below layers of unforgiveness. Each hidden pain must be brought to the surface, to face your presence and to be forgiven, taking you a step closer to salvation.

As your practice of forgiveness gathers momentum, it soon turns into a gigantic rolling snowball effect until, eventually, you forgive continually and the salvation of your multiverse and our world is complete.

As you reach the end of your journey and have forgiven away all your earthly pain and judgement, God takes you by the hand, cloaks you with His Holy Spirit, and leads you into Heaven Himself.

Chapter 7

We don't need no body!

It does not matter whether we have missing limbs, loss of eyesight, or anything we think of as bodily. We are not a body or a thing. Our earthly bodies are the illusory external appearance of our earthly pain body, the culmination of all our doubts. It is not even about closing our eyes and meditating. In truth, we do not even have a head. Everything is illusion.

Our worries create only illusions, including our earthly bodies. In truth, we are formless.

So be nothing and rest in gratitude, forgiveness, acceptance and joy, and reach Heaven's Gate, whereupon God will make the last step and you will know His love for eternity.

Imagine salvation as escaping through your mind. Instead of imperfect thoughts that will only show you the imperfect earth, you have perfect thoughts – God's thoughts – that show you a perfect world and the truth of what you are in Him. This is salvation: when you have given up your will for God's Will, and given up all earthly thoughts for God's Thoughts only.

So calm your fears, do not worry about the past or the future, forgive continually all your doubts, and trust God's Thoughts will come into your mind to make your perfect world.

Chapter 8

Unforgiveness, the cross we carry

Remember always to consistently and continually share and give your gratitude and your love, remembering that our love comes from our oneness in Christ God and is limitless. Our unconditional love will pour onto everything we create as we gaze upon our multiverse with gratitude, forgiveness, acceptance and non-judgement, our world blessed and saved by our love.

Consistently give thanks rather than sadness. Like the poorest of the poor who smile and look upon their world in happiness, know love instead, and know it comes from Christ God. Most of us are blocked by layers of seemingly complicated illusory worries and miss the beauty in our lives, our smiling children, and other people's outpouring of love on the world and each other. Salvation is here and now, everywhere and in everything, if we could just remove the blinkers covering our minds, replacing our fears and hate with our unconditional love.

Those who know and accept that Christ God lives in them as one, and who know through experience that all their joy and happiness is a direct consequence of His felt loving presence, understand that He is the door that gives escape from the illusory hell we once thought had no exit.

The cause of your unhappiness is that you forget and identify yourself, your being, with that of an illusory earth-bound body, bound by chains of unforgiveness and judgement, weighing you and your brother down, trapped in a self-made prison you built.

Do not hold onto unforgiveness; it leads to strange thoughts like "Why do bad things happen to good people?" or "Why do bad things not happen to wicked people?" All these comparisons and thoughts only lead your awareness deeper into suffering and pain. Instead, your energies are better spent on expressing your gratitude and love generously on your forgiven world, forgiven continually by yourself, its saviour, whereupon you will truly perceive joy as you give thanks to God in oneness.

So no longer hold yourselves, others and the entire earth prisoner. Instead, set the world, others and yourself free in God's perfect plan with your forgiveness, non-judgement, gratitude and acceptance of His love for us all without exception.

The instant of our salvation is Christ God arriving with His unconditional love, His blessings falling like gentle rain on our dried-out, loveless, barren world, lighting up every living and non-living thing with heavenly peace and love. It is like the mothership returning at last to seemingly lost souls drifting through time without any means of communication.

Live in your world without judging, accepting, and giving forgiveness continually through God's love to all your creation, without prejudice or any kind of judgement.

We should not feel entitled to anger, malice or revenge, for God has already given us everything He has for mankind. If we lived in continual gratitude, we would see the world anew, with love in every living and non-living thing, a place of heavenly beauty.

Every moment and every situation, we have a choice to live in heaven with forgiveness, gratitude and Christ Vision, or in hell with resentment, ingratitude and darkness.

Know through experience that gratitude to our Creator is gratitude to our multiverse and to each other, the source of our completion and eternal love and peace. God is incomplete without our love for Him and each other.

Chapter 9

Save your Self with your unconditional love

We crucify ourselves with anger and hate, or we save ourselves with unconditional love.

Immediately after our creation, we feared ourselves and the world we found ourselves in. In doing so, because we are created One in God, we feared God at the same time. The goal of our journey home is not to fear ourselves and, at the same time, not to fear God, but to love Him instead. It is for us to find and accept His unconditional love, which we can only do if we give our love to everything and everyone we perceive. God loves everyone and everything He creates. It is on us to be like Him and to love everything and everyone we perceive, so that we may know His eternal unconditional love.

In an attempt to shake off fear, like any animal would try to do, we project our anger and all our negative emotions at everything and everyone around us.

In truth, our beingness is gifted in Christ God as One. We are the creators of everything we perceive. Therefore, we need to remember that, rather than projecting our fears onto our perceived outer world, we should instead negate it, cancelling the pain and anxieties of fear with forgiveness, allowing our love, born of forgiveness, to shine upon all of our creations.

Chapter 10

We create the Gifts we give to ourselves

We are the creators of our own lives and multiverse. As such, we gift everything through our creativity to ourselves. We are both the creative giver and the creative receiver. We give and receive love at the same time.

To avoid falling into the trap of ingratitude when your gift to others seemingly is not received in gratitude (you feel their ingratitude), immediately remember that you have given the gift to yourself. Therefore, it is you who should be, and is, grateful. Successfully transacted, you remain in Christ Vision instead of descending once again into hell.

In other words, do not let earthly negative emotional feelings take over your beingness (do not let the coin land tails up), as you remember that you create and gift to yourself everything in your multiverse. Remain in Christ God with Christ Vision, heads up always, as you interact with your own multiverse creation your mother, your partner, your friend, your enemy, and everyone in your life.

So, each time, remember: when you forgive, you forgive yourself. When you give, you give to yourself. When you love, you love yourself.

When you interact with your creation, learn to remember that you interact with your Self, the Craftsman's Apprentice. Continuously remember that you have been gifted your multiverse in its entirety. Do not split it into fragments with temptations, judgements, prejudice, or ingratitude, becoming a small thing, falling down a rabbit hole of fear and turning Wonderland into hell and madness.

Instead, keep it simple and accept, with complete gratitude, the entire universe you have been gifted. Be grateful that you already have been given everything Christ in God has. Your ingratitude prevents you from experiencing every heavenly gift now.

Continually use your limitless willpower and courage, and do not allow the embryonic earth and its perceptions to drag your mind away into its worrisome thoughts and expectations. Instead, expect nothing, trust God, live in the present moment, and continue to calm your being. Be grateful to yourself that your consistent forgiveness, in your oneness with God, is limitless and holds the power to negate any perceived madness that earthly thoughts may conjure up, instantly replacing them with Christ Vision your perfect multiverse, Heaven.

For example, when you look after a friend's child and the child acts up, appearing ungrateful, and the friend likewise appears unappreciative and negative, remember that the whole episode is your creation. It is your multiverse, and you are the cause. It is you in the friend, you in the child, you in you. Forgive away any pain, forgive yourself in all living things, refocus, and simply remain in gratitude as you create your multiverse in its corrected heavenly form. Do not put yourself under worry or pressure about what you will say or do. Just forgive and let be, with love, what will be in your multiverse in Christ God.

Chapter 11

Everything perceived is illusion except forgiveness

Everything is illusion. Every illusion, except forgiveness, leads to more illusions. Forgiveness removes our pain and directs us back to Our Creator, never to more illusions. Forgiveness, practiced continually, leads to the transmutation of all anxieties and pain and is the last stepping stone before looking upon our world in freedom anew, in Oneness with Christ God, for eternity with Unconditional Love.

The Veil between Heaven and Embryonic Earth is made of unforgiveness.

You could be the most powerful, the richest, the most evil, the poorest, or the most destitute individual. It does not matter. You will still be stuck in the pain of temptation here in hell, trapped until you understand and continually exercise the healing and loving power of forgiveness upon all your creations and all your perceptions.

Your freedom, your true Self in Christ God, will only be known to you when you continually and unconditionally exercise your loving forgiveness. Either way, Christ God will be your Saviour. The question is, how much suffering do you wish to endure before His arrival, His Presence in you?

Draw from your unlimited store of willpower and courage, and continuously exercise loving forgiveness on your anxieties and suffering. Prevent illusionary thoughts from dragging you away from the present moment.

Rather than allow temptation to provide meagre relief from your suffering, exercise one hundred percent forgiveness and block every doubting thought and illusion that causes your separation from Oneness in Christ God.

Continually exercise forgiveness and non-judgement, and know your multiverse in Heaven's truth, your Home, and not your living hell.

Continual, unconditional, loving forgiveness is the narrow door, the only key to your freedom and salvation in Christ God.

Chapter 12

We are no thing!

We are nothing. In truth, we are mind. Without the illusionary ego's thoughts and the illusory bodily creation they produce, we would know this to be true.

Your goal is for your will to be one with God's Will, to triumph over the ego's illusionary thoughts and hate. Triumphant, your awareness is home in the Oneness of its Creator's love.

The ego will trick you with its illusionary, fear-driven thoughts into believing your home is the body it created. Instead, stay the course. Your willpower is unlimited, and you will know salvation in your real home, which is your mind, free from embryonic earthly thoughts and your illusory ego.

Once you fully practice being in full awareness with your Creator, the body's only purpose becomes an instrument for the Holy Spirit in the plan its Creator has mapped out. Remember to distinguish between "living" living in the bodily, ego-driven death and "just being," which is living in God's Oneness through continual acceptance and forgiveness.

Free of worrisome thoughts, witness your acceptance of God's gifts upon your transmuted multiverse as you continually and consistently practise forgiveness. Find freedom in God's Oneness as you escape through the veil of unforgiveness.

Your illusionary body's sole purpose is to follow truth and to seek mankind's salvation through freedom found in the union of mind with its Creator's Thoughts.

As all minds are connected, your salvation is mankind's salvation. As mankind witnesses your truth in God, it is instantly transformed. Cloaked in the Holy Spirit, the Love of God flows freely to all mankind, transforming all minds through salvation.

Your realisation in truth that you are mind and not a body is your freedom from slavery and salvation in Christ God.

Chapter 13

Peace is our journeys end

Peace will only be found at the journey's end.

It is remembering that the road to hell is wide and full of temptation, which will delay us, hold us prisoner, and lead to more and more dead-end detours, temptations, false idols, and so on.

Our mind's thoughts need to change.

This can only be achieved when we realise that true peace is Oneness in Christ God and by allowing His thoughts to replace our primitive thoughts. By trusting, accepting, and being open-minded, we receive God's thoughts and truth, revealing His Plan for us.

Forgiveness enables us to shake off old patterns, but only a change of thoughts beyond forgiveness accepting God's Thoughts, practiced continually will free us from bondage. In other words, accept your multiverse and everything God would have you learn, but remember not to attach to any of it for comfort. Attach only to God's Love, whilst giving it freely to your multiverse at the same time. Do not be tricked into resting where there are only thorns. Remove the thorns, forgive them away before you rest; the anxieties and the pains must be released with your loving forgiveness.

With your willpower, keep striving to live in God's peace instead, expecting the least, grasping nothing, and trusting in Him to continually gift the power of loving forgiveness that you can perceive in Christ Vision.

Chapter 14
God is in all of us

It's as if God, as He created each of us, put a small piece of His awareness into us so He could experience what it is like, experientially, to be us.

Not just us, but every living and non-living thing, everything and everyone.

He is the whole, complete awareness of everything in the Cosmos.

My thoughts are that salvation is the return of each bit of His awareness to the Whole, to Himself.

Or put another way, in our own individual lives, our own multiverse, being one in Him, we return to the Whole of Him when we, in the illusion, are about to reach the end of His script.

In other words, our salvation is God putting the lights on when the play, the movie, is about to end.

It is like being chaperoned to the cinema by you in Him whilst in the body of a fictional you.

So the real lesson here is that we absolutely do not have anything to worry about. The earth, our bodies, how we lived our lives none of it matters because God's plan knows our lesson was His lesson: to know what it is to be us. He had, at the beginning, already established His and our escape route, our salvation, which is to return to the Whole of Himself.

It makes me think about people who experience near-death and talk about how they did not want to return to earth as their bodies lay on the operating table. They all speak of how it was explained to them by spirit, an agreement, a sort of contract to live and be in the host they inhabit on earth, and that the time is not yet right to go to Heaven, but soon they will return to Heavenly peace.

So here, our small piece of awareness, although we forget, will return to the Whole of Awareness at some point. Because we, the children of God, belong to the Whole of Awareness, all of God.

Also, we seemingly have a separate part our own free will that will choose salvation when the time and situation finally arrive, because God Himself, being part of ourselves, chooses it for us and Himself, the Oneness that is us.

Chapter 15

Christ Gods love is unconditional

Christ God's love is unconditional and unlimited.

Always remember that your real home is love. It is not a place external to you; it is knowing yourself in Christ God. It is a perfect state of feeling and being.

You always, of course, have the potential to be angry and full of hatred, but with your ability to forgive, accept, be indefensive, and give, you always have the option to train yourself to look at those triggers differently and escape the depressing patterns you keep repeating.

All you need to do is love yourself and everything that you perceive by knowing, understanding, and truly believing that you exist in Oneness in Christ God. Therefore, you are given freely unlimited amounts of His and your unconditional Love, to give freely to everyone and everything in your Multiverse and to change everything perceived by you in Christ God for your own and the entire world's salvation.

So just be happy, remembering always that all you need to do is freely accept and give love continually, while at the same time being strong-willed and not allowing that perfect state of being to be interrupted by worrisome, hateful, or angry judgements and patterns of behaviour.

Chapter 16

Salvation's only obstacle is me

Salvation's only obstacle is me and my non-acceptance. This led me to ask, why do I not accept salvation? This led me to note the following.

Remember always, it is not that thing, that person, or that event that is upsetting your happiness, but it is you allowing it to happen in the first place by stepping out of love, out of integrity, and by not continually allowing love to pour through your being into your perceptions, your creation, your Multiverse. Remember always, "you are the projector," and as such you can project anything you want from your and Christ God's unlimited store. So project love always.

By stepping out of love and integrity, you perceive your brothers, sisters, and everything else through the lenses of illusory fears you have attached to, with anger and hate, which your ego grasps onto for its imaginary battle for survival, and which it projects onto your screen, overlaying the image your love in Christ God would project otherwise.

Your natural state of integrity is love. You are love. Love is your home.

When you become attached or fearful of that event, that person, or that thing, you have projected fear into your Multiverse. You have become lost in its world, the embryonic earth, the ancient home of our embryonic ancestors.

Unglue yourself and transmute all your fears with loving forgiveness, and keep doing the same with all unforgiveness still hiding or residing in your pain, your anxieties, and your being, hiding behind temptations.

Remember not to doubt. Continually love, always, no matter what you perceive.

Be the head, not the tail. Do not let fear take over and control you. Just be yourself, the master, and continually take courage from your and Christ God's unlimited store. Christ God is always in you, so allow His love to pour through you and into your creation, into your world.

Perceive continually all your Multiverse, your world, with your unconditional, unlimited love in Christ God, and witness the washing away of all perceived sins before you with its miraculous transformative power, turning your Multiverse or hell into your Multiverse or Heaven.

Baptise yourself with Christ God's Love.

If you find yourself lost, upset, miserable, or unloved, simply remember to continually give love, to lovingly forgive, to not doubt, to not judge, to accept, and to feel your love in Christ God flow again. Witness its miraculous power as it unshackles you, everyone, and everything you perceive, which you would otherwise hold prisoner.

Chapter 17

We are not bound by earthly laws

We are not bound by earthly laws.

True freedom, peace, and well-being can only be experienced when living in union with Christ God.

In this state of mind, with Christ God's and your own love flowing, your world of illusions is powerless to resist miraculous transformation, turning your former hell into your present Heaven.

Think how the early Christians must have lived, having received Jesus's teaching more or less first-hand, either from Himself or through the earliest believers. They would undoubtedly have been awash in the love of Christ God after accepting His outpouring of loving forgiveness.

Imagine them living then, having received and understood clear, simple instructions. No books, no dilution of the truth, knowing how to rid themselves of illusionary earthly worries and be free to receive their heavenly multiverse paradise.

For the ruling authorities trapped in their illusory world, those early Christians were no longer controllable and an absolute nightmare to govern, whilst their numbers grew rapidly each day.

Not caring about taxes or interested in anything their former illusory world had to offer them then or in the future, the more they were persecuted and terrorised, the further into Christ Love they went. Jesus's message was as simple as it gets: continually, consistently, and lovingly forgive everything in their illusory multiverse and let their love in Christ God flow to sustain them, their heavenly inheritance through Him earned because of their continual unconditional loving forgiveness.

For the poor, the choice was obvious: to have nothing in the illusion of hell of our embryonic ancestors, or to have freedom in Christ God and have everything.

Imagine their beautiful, shining faces as they were each nailed to the cross, millions already living in paradise. Their crucifixion was as meaningless to them as everything else they had left behind in their illusory world.

They chose instead, with their courage, to overcome fear with their loving forgiveness and to live in Christ God's Love, in Eternal Life itself, their awareness transported into paradise before the death of their illusory body.

Chapter 18

Creating a space for inserting Gods Divine Thought

Remember, willpower is the mind exercising separation from the illusory world and the illusionary primitive thoughts and doubt it would create. It is like creating a gap in a strand of DNA and making space for inserting God's Divine Thought to create a miracle. The result is always brilliance: a new Olympic record, renewed faith, or a child taking its first walking step.

Willpower is also tangible proof that the mind is separate from thoughts and the body.

For example, in training to excel at anything, such as running, fasting, tennis, combat soldiering, or practising your faith in persecution, your aim is to practice continually until you succeed without fearing death, overcoming your body's and thoughts' resistance.

That is why Jesus was thankful to God for making it easier for the meek and humble, mostly the poor and destitute, to enter His and our Father's house.

Think about it. With destitution comes daily fear of death, right in front of you. Given this knowledge and understanding, all the meek had then, and have now, to do is see the gap in their minds a space for God's Thoughts, which was already a mile wide because of their trials and tribulations.

Successfully exercised, your willpower will detach and triumph over its illusionary body and thoughts every time.

It is just that, because willpower was not exercised, the mind could never see a gap, a difference between itself and the illusory body and thoughts to which its awareness would normally be attached.

Always remember that your mind is separate from your earthly thoughts and everything it perceives, whether it is illusory hell or truth and home.

Exercise continually, with your ever-increasing willpower, non-judgement, and forgiveness, and free yourself from the looping primitive thoughts of our embryonic ancestors and the temptations that would drag you into their embryonic world. Without exercising willpower, you are easily stuck in patterns the wide door to hell.

With the separation of mind from your body's thoughts, a gap and a space to insert God's Thoughts appear. From this comes peace and creation, your mind in Oneness with Christ God the narrow door to Heaven and your protection in the Holy Spirit.

Because you have created a gap, a separation between earthly thoughts and your willpower, you can now witness and be aware of your mind, free to create in union with Christ God as He fills the gap you created in your mind with His shared Thoughts.

Chapter 19

You are the projector not the screen

Our true selves, the witness of everything we create, experience, and know of, remain forever undamaged and sinless.

The Father cannot fairly punish His children for playing and watching the movies He created and left unlocked in His video cabinet.

Heartfelt gratitude can only be known by your true self when your love is given and felt by your true self. It is difficult to be my true self, to be grateful to my true self, and to love my true self because of the obstacles, the temptations, and the judgments I create in my multiverse.

Only your true self can give your true self salvation. Salvation cannot come from anything you create, including your body, your ego, a drug, or someone or something else. Everything is your creation. It is like expecting the image on a movie screen to fix the broken film projector. It is never going to happen.

The projector, your true self, can change only the movie that is played. It can play a happy movie, a funny comedy, or a nightmare. Its willpower alone determines what is played and what is created.

But the best movie you can play and feel is God's Love, your love, His gratitude one with yours, when you surrender, surrender to His Will. Give thanks to Him, be One in Him, and let you in Him fix your life, your salvation, and His thoughts one with yours, and it will be the greatest movie ever played.

Chapter 20

We condemn ourselves

We condemn ourselves with the judgements we place upon our embryonic multiverse. Stored pent-up anger, hatred, and unforgiveness all reduce your multiverse to a miserable imprisonment, full of dark perceptions and unhappiness, where condemnation condemns only ourselves.

We must each take ownership of our own lives, our own multiverse.

Your goal must be to remain focused on the salvation of your multiverse, to look through the veil with Christ's vision, and see through the darkness of your multiverse. We are all our own saviours, the light that turns darkness into heaven.

Temptation leads to attachments, judgement, and condemnation, like sticky glue, slowing you down on your path.

Continual forgiveness breaks down attachments, like thinners breaking down the adhesion of the glue of your earthly multiverse. This allows you to pass quickly through the veil with Christ's vision, keeping your course straight.

Chapter 21

We are formless

We are all creators of our lives, our Multiverses, and yet we remain no-thing. Our bodies are just another one of our creations, which we witness each day, created in our minds. You could say our earthly bodies are equivalent to the neighbour's cat, the cup you drink from, the ink in the book you read, or the breeze on your illusory face illusions created in our mind by earthly thoughts.

If anything, we are more akin to cosmic creatures projecting creations of light from our minds, the background of the No-thing we are.

We are God's children, possessing many of His attributes. Like Him, we are no-thing. We are formless, the witness, the creator; we are mind, as is He.

Meditation stills the mind, allowing new thoughts and Christ Vision. By letting go of illusion, by meditating, not worrying, and calming our emotions, we are free to release fear and pent-up frustrations.

Our life's goal is to be continuously in meditation, escaping from darkness our minds create, making room for new thoughts, God's thoughts. In meditation, we aim for one goal: One mind, in union with God's mind, and one Vision, His and our Vision, Christ God Vision as One.

Trust God to lead with His thoughts, and know and experience that we are His children.

We are the light of creation in God, with the ability to witness dark illusions or Christ Vision. Our minds can look upon earthly illusions or, through acceptance, non-judgement, and forgiveness, experience heavenly happiness.

Clarity of vision comes with a strengthened union of mind with our Creator. Refreshed and rested, we are free to create and witness with more courage, able to transmute hidden fears through courage rather than through temptation.

Transmutation of fear through forgiveness and non-judgement leads to acceptance and gratitude, transforming dark illusions with the light of Christ Vision into our heavenly multiverse, our inheritance. Metaphorically speaking, it is like a coin, seeing God's thoughts heads up with the face of God and not tails, the tail of the devil, or earthly embryonic thoughts.

Chapter 22

We are mind with free will

We need to believe that we are mind and not body. The body and everything we perceive are constantly being created in our minds for us to know through perceived experience.

Because we are mind, with free will, we have the freedom to think of anything and everything we wish. However, there is an earthly trap that keeps us prisoner in the perceptions we have created. These are non-acceptance, judgement, and unforgiveness, masked by temptation. Temptation is like a double lock, the ropes wrapped around twice. Until we break free, there is no peace to be had, as the emotions of our embryonic ancestors overwhelm us in our perceptions.

Peace is achieved only when you follow God's thoughts with your mind. Your mind is no longer paralysed by earthly thoughts, temptations, non-acceptance, anger, hate, unforgiveness, or judgements.

We are free to be one mind, sharing God's thoughts in peace and love.

Chapter 23
Created in Gods Mind

Distracted by our own creations, our perceptions, and our multiverse, we forget that we are created in God's mind, just as our creations are created in our minds.

If you block out everything, every earthly thought, in meditation for example, bringing your mind to peace and stillness whilst seeking God's thoughts, a conversation of minds becomes possible. In that stillness, you pause your multiverse from producing its usual story. In other words, you could say that you freeze your multiverse and find peace for a while.

Chapter 24

The ego steps aside

The ego host, with faith and discipline, whilst not fully understanding who the Son of God is, can trust and fully support Him with its illusionary body and thoughts. To such an extent, the ego is prepared to step aside and trust in Him fully, offering its will and allowing the Son of God to play a full and active supportive role in its being, for the salvation not only of itself but of the whole of its world.

From the perspective of the Son of God, who lives in all of us, it has found another door into the whole world, another source of light, for the salvation of itself and everyone, and to make itself whole and complete.

Chapter 25

Everything mistaken thoughts

Our seeming bodies are just distractions, a product of our mistaken thoughts, or, as I would say, thoughts of embryonic mankind of a separated mind. Our real life is in God's mind and God's mind only, with His shared thoughts, without the distraction of embryonic earthly thoughts.

Remember, our true self is spirit and mind, a part of God's spirit and mind, and not of this earthly world or our illusory earthly bodies.

Our only goal is to live continually in God's mind without the distraction of the embryonic earth, continually acknowledging that our true home is our One Mind with His Thoughts only.

Having conquered fear and resting in God, His and our Thoughts are one and the same. Christ is sinless and our aspiration, a goal for ourselves, having achieved and remembered equal sinless status, having cleared our minds of earthly thoughts and temptations. We no longer look upon a sinful world as our minds are co-joined with Christ God's mind.

Our minds remain trapped on earth and lonely because we forget who we are, having accepted embryonic earthly thoughts in place of

God's thoughts, prolonging our imprisonment through temptation, judgement, non-acceptance, ingratitude, and lack of forgiveness.

We share God's name when we are no longer separated from Him: Father and Son as One Living Being in God's true home.

In summary, our minds have simply forgotten who we really are as we remain preoccupied with earthly fear and temptations. Temptation can be thought of as pain relief for our suffering whilst living the lives of our embryonic ancestors. While engaged in temptation, we will always be lost in earthly thoughts and a million miles from our home in Christ God.

Only because we have forgotten are we imprisoned in the alien world of our embryonic ancestors.

And so, the only way to return our mind to Heaven, its home, is to remind it continually to resist temptation and its associated thoughts through forgiveness of pain and non-judgement, the price that must be paid for salvation.

Chapter 26

Magic dust

Eventually, through continual acceptance of the gift of heavenly forgiveness for ourselves and others in our multiverse, we shall learn to pass through the veil between heaven and earth.

Forgiveness is like magic dust that dissolves the veil that surrounds and blinds us to our Heaven.

Remember to give the forgiveness you are given to your multiverse so that it transforms into heaven.

Remember, like anything else, you must accept forgiveness in order to give it. Do not try to give a poor earthly version of it.

Like everything stored for you in Heaven, you must receive to give, as you give to receive more.

In a worrisome mind here on earth, we have nothing. Forgiveness is non-existent. Its resemblance, at best, is to ignore certain forms of behaviour and force a smile upon your grieving face.

Heaven's forgiveness is unparalleled in scope and power.

So continually love your life. Accept and give heavenly forgiveness until it flows through you like a heavenly stream. You will never forget your Father or feel lost or unloved whilst doing so.

As your former illusory prison fades away, you will know God's benevolence and truth directly in His house.

Imagine being a persecuted Christian, each day having your buttons pressed to get a reaction and distract you from your path.

The poor were taught by Jesus to ignore bad treatment by others and divert their energies instead to accepting and giving more and more forgiveness so they could give it to the world they inhabited and bless their tormentors with it. Extending their forgiveness to their enemies, their being would be filled with the Holy Spirit, and filled with more forgiveness and love.

So, like the ant kicking away at the elephant's foot, their enemies' blows had no effect on them. Millions of Christ's followers had risen above their earthly situations to their higher self in Christ God, protected in the peace of the Holy Spirit. They stood tall above it all, smiling like Buddha as the flames lapped at their feet and the blood drained from their upside-down bodies, nailed to the cross.

In summary, our goal is to light up our world by becoming an Olympic gold medallist in non-judgement, receiving and giving forgiveness to ourselves and everything we look upon in our multiverse.

Chapter 27
Love is natural

A good example of love is our children. We accept that we created them at an earthly level and have no problem with our simple earthly circulating thoughts reminding us of this.

Love comes naturally in this case. We accept them in our awareness, and we are at peace when they behave around us. We take for granted the feeling of love we have for them. We do not question it.

Imagine nature's evolution. To achieve its preferred outcome, which is the perfection of its work, every species and all of nature's creations must evolve. If love is the go sign, the thumbs up, its happiness with the outcome, then forgiveness is the stop sign, the thumbs down, signalling that it wants no more of this or that. Yes, I want more of that; alternatively, no, I do not want more of that. Love and forgiveness are both nature's decisions, and as God created nature, all these decisions are also His decisions.

Imagine then nature in God having completed all its tasks of evolving every species, including our own. The route to that point involved zillions upon zillions of love and forgiveness decisions.

The mind of God, the Master Craftsman at work, has made each and every one of those decisions.

Given that we are co-creators with nature and that God is the driving force of all creation, all of nature, it follows that we need only accept forgiveness, follow forgiveness to follow love, and give love to marvel at God's work, all God's creations, including ourselves. Love through forgiveness will reveal the best version of all of God's creations.

In other words, to be in God, we need only accept, receive, and give His and our love to all His creations. Why His and our love? Because that is God's decision: to make everything a part of Him, in His being. In other words, God continually creates Himself; He absorbs all of His creations within Him.

For our earthly minds, judgement takes us to love or hate decisions. We must be no different from the Master Craftsman and change our attitude to love and forgiveness decisions. The decision is ours. However, if our multiverse is already created perfect as Christ God taught and has been from the beginning of our creation, we need not judge. We need only love, forgive, and marvel at His and our creation to be in Heavenly love continually.

On an earthly level, we think we did not create our pets, yet we are able to accept and feel love for them as well. On an earthly level, we think we did not create our enemies, yet we know we can love them too. Proof that love can be accepted and given to our children and pets, but also accepted and given to our enemies.

If forgiveness is the effort to get on the kite surfboard, then love is the wind that sustains the journey. In other words, love accepted and given is the prize for the effort made. The effort is acceptance, non-judgement, gratitude, and forgiveness.

Love needs no earthly thoughts to sustain it. Unlike its opposite, hate, love is peace of mind.

We return our love to God by continually trusting, accepting that His and our co-created perfect decisions have been made already with love, and trusting that everything in our multiverse created is already made perfect by forgiveness and love.

Remember, the instant we accept hate, we see imperfection, and the veil drops down like a steel shutter.

In summary, we in God are the beginning and the end of evolution, and we in Him have already made all perfect decisions, all perfect judgements that brought us to our creation in Him. His and our love, then, as the Master Craftsman, must be the direction, the road to Him.

Therefore, we need only accept and give love to live in Him and find our true selves. When we accept His and our love and gift it to all things in our multiverse, we give everything and everyone, in effect, the map, the route home. Also, in love, we rest and marvel at His perfect creation, and in your being in Him, you marvel at your own creation.

In other words, rest, accept, and simply marvel, and love your creation. In the same way you love your children, love all things, for in all things are the works of God and your true self.

Trust God and yourself as co-creators. Everything made with love in your multiverse is the result of correct decisions made by you in God.

In other words, train your mind to trust, love, and see everything as perfect in your multiverse, as God has made all the right decisions already for your world to be perfect.

Chapter 28
Love is what I am

Love is what I am.

Everything in my multiverse is stuff to know of, in my mind, my creation. None of it is me. None of it is my true essence.

Thoughts are stuff to know of, but none of it is me. If anything, I am the projector; I am not the screen or the image.

Do not worry about anything occurring in your multiverse, on the screen. Forgive away the associated pain and detach from the screen and the image.

None of it is you, even when you think it is. You think it is you when you allow circulating thoughts to roam free in your mind unchecked. You attach to the pain of unforgiven thoughts.

Release yourself from the primitive thoughts that torment and create the illusionary multiverse that blinds your true vision in Christ God. Let it all go.

You grasp onto it by holding the pain. Forgive away all the pain. Detach from the pain by not judging, by accepting, and by forgiving the pain away. Breathe in, then let it go.

Let it all pass through you. Let the whole illusion pass you by. Allow non-judgement, acceptance, and forgiveness to be your Teflon armour, shielding you from the veil that would imprison you in the embryonic world and the human bodies of our cosmic ancestors.

Give thanks to their world of illusions and sacrifice, and move on. Detach with forgiveness from your pain body and let it go.

Instead of pain, feel and accept, through forgiveness, the love of Christ God, and be free in Him, your true self, and home.

Chapter 29
My thoughts are not my own

I am mind.

I accept earthly thoughts.

My thoughts are not me; they are thoughts I can choose to accept or reject. Earthly thoughts create fear, images, sounds, smells, feelings, and everything in my perception the embryonic earth and embryonic mankind that which I am still attached to. Everything I am attached to is engaging my mind. I am a prisoner of my earthly thoughts.

My thoughts of the embryonic earth are holding me hostage in a self-made, self-imposed exile, separated from my true home in Christ God.

I need to accept that this is what I am. I am mind, and my earthly body is simply the perceived result of earthly thoughts I accepted separately from God. I do not really have an earthly body or anybody in the dream of illusions I mistakenly called my home.

I am mind only, creating my illusionary body with borrowed thoughts, creating other bodies and other objects with borrowed thoughts. Everything is thought. It does not mean I have to accept the pattern of thoughts and associated images producing the "so-called life" I have created.

I can leave the whole light show my mind has created by changing my thoughts. By trusting and accepting God's thoughts and returning to Him, my home, I am free from separation and whole in Him, our mind in Oneness.

If I have no embryonic earthly thoughts, my mind defaults to stillness, and in that stillness, peace.

How can I have the thoughts that produce pure happiness and not the world of pure suffering of embryonic mankind? The answer is to end my separation and trust, living in One Mind in Christ God.

In truth, I am just mind, never in reality separated from my Creator. Like Him, my mind needs to let everything, the world of illusions go. Let my mind have nothing to do in the world of illusions projected by my borrowed thoughts. Every thought I have thought has been "loaned" from the "book of mankind" and belongs to a time long gone zillions upon zillions of years ago. Not that time existed then or now either. Time, like everything else, is another illusion mistakenly perceived through earthly judgements, as is the rest of the illusion.

All the arguments and all the stress my mind has experienced have been the result of loaned thoughts from a time long ago. What I think of that which is God is the same; they are borrowed thoughts.

All of my cherished beliefs are simply borrowed thoughts my earthly body has accepted as "its truth".

The real truth is that all the truths from the thoughts I accepted create illusions, projections, or "translations" on my mind, my seemingly fragmented mind.

I want to know peace. The only path to peace in truth is when my fragmented, seemingly separated mind is still.

Once my mind is still and knows peace, it will know to accept its Creator's thoughts.

I should be happy now that I know I am not this light show, which I thought was my life. It is time for me to go home. It is time to go home to my one whole mind, one in my Creator's mind, and know everlasting peace in His shared thoughts.

Chapter 30

We are not in our right minds

Reminder, we are mind, not a body, not a human brain as we know it.

Mind is something much greater.

Most of the time, we are not in our right minds. We are in our brains, lost in primitive thoughts.

When we are in our right minds, we are one with God's Mind.

As long as we see the imperfect illusory world we seemingly inhabit with our illusory bodies in unhappiness, we are lost in embryonic brain thoughts and deep behind the veil.

Our minds always have a choice to leave the world of illusions, leave our own condemnation at any instant, and become aware instead of God's House, God's Mind, and God's shared Thoughts.

It is for our minds to understand how to make the switch, and then make its own decision by utilising its free will to do so.

Our free will is our mind's choice to "want to know of".

I want to know God's House instead of the world of illusions I have made. Is my mind wanting to know my mind shared with God's Mind and His shared thoughts?

So exercise your free will, your mind, your choice, and your desire to know through forgiveness and non-judgement God's shared Mind.

Want to know what it is like to accept and give away, to forgive all earthly troublesome thoughts, and release your mind to receive God's silent peaceful thought in Oneness of Mind.

Passing through the veil of illusions is like trying to run through a gooey swamp.

Wanting to know the truth without judgment gives the mind the power to run.

Forgiveness provides the mind the power to leap.

Both together give the power to run above the surface of the veil and rise up into God's Mind.

So, in your daily life experience, continually want to know without judgement whilst forgiving away any residual pain, and transform your daily life into God's Mind.

Chapter 31

Unforgiven thoughts blind us to love

The Holy Spirit just wants us to be our true selves.

Every unforgiven thought blinds us to love, our true identity, revealing not what God has kept in store for us, but instead an imperfect world of illusions created by embryonic earthly thoughts entering our unguarded minds.

Unforgiveness is unsettling, like emotional waves on the seashore, mixing crystal-clear waters with sand, blinding God's truth and creating our judgments and the heavy pain bodies we carry.

Only forgiveness can dissolve our pain and filter out our judgments, revealing our peace, our unconditional love, and the limitless ocean of love we, in our Creator, can gift.

Chapter 32

Loving peace

We need to return to what we are, that is, loving peace. It is upon us to continually perceive with love and peace everything contained within our embryonic ancestry, our ancestral planet Earth, and the universe.

Our Creator loves us and His creations. Our love is His gifted love. As we give love, we give His love to our entire multiverse.

If you feel worrisome, continually forgive and forgive more, your multiverse and everything in your awareness, including yourself, until you have recaptured and refocused the love gifted from our Creator in the present, free of worries about the future or the past.

With practice, you will become an expert, continually expressing your love and true self, one with our Father.

As you do, your salvation in God, in His Oneness, is secured. With this, God's loving peace flows into your multiverse and into the whole world.

Your continual love of your multiverse is the channel that pours salvation upon the entire world, every living thing in it.

The whole world's salvation awaits your salvation through your love.

It is like watching, in loving peace, a ten-thousand-year-old movie reel of yourself and your world. It can never harm you as long as you watch and are aware of it in loving peace, in the protection of the Holy Spirit.

In other words, your loving peace has banished fear through your continual forgiveness, taming your multiverse to more loving peace, forever in your awareness.

Love is awareness, the giver of life. You are alive because I am aware of you. I am alive because you are aware of me.

In other words, love creates from Wholeness. Your love is the creator of your world.

Your whole world takes ownership of itself when your loving peace flows through you.

Love and peace are the currency that creates.

Forgiveness is the price we pay for love and peace so we can create.

Chapter 33
Remember God

Remember God, we have forgotten our Father's Love and forgotten Heaven; we are lost.

We are lost in the veil, in an ocean of earthly thoughts. Lost meaning that we do not understand.

Once you know something, it is impossible to unknow it. Let us assume there is something we still do not fully understand and that, when understood completely, will provide the key to returning to God.

Then perhaps that which we do not understand is that there is nothing else to know, and the journey ends. Heaven, God, appears the instant you stop seeking, when you stop thinking earthly thoughts. Just be, just rest, and create space in your mind for God's thoughts. Merge into your Father as One, with His shared thoughts, He who knows and understands everything, having created everything already.

The thing to be understood is to stop thinking with earthly thoughts, to stop searching, to accept, to not judge, and in gratitude to our ancient cosmic ancestors, forgive away every pain you carry from them, and every one of their ancient thoughts. Let them rest in peace. Let yourself rest in peace.

In doing so, you will find and rest forever in God's Love, where they rest and wait in God for your return.

Chapter 34

Put your faith in Gods thoughts

Put your faith in God's thoughts, His shared thoughts, as opposed to worrisome, fearful thoughts of illusory embryonic mankind received on your unguarded mind.

Hourly, and continually if you can, remember not to judge, to be thankful, accepting, forgiving, and giving of God's love throughout the day. Keep yourself focused on your true self in Christ God instead of your illusory, seemingly separated self in embryonic mankind, thinking earthly thoughts.

Imagine a perfect day in a holiday destination in the Son, time felt and spent in the real You, in Christ God's love. Your existence resting perfectly, wanting for nothing.

All knowledge sought by your illusory self is an anthill in comparison to the mountain of truth available when trusting your mind to shared mind-thoughts in Christ God. Put your faith and trust in God.

Our fearful self hates the idea of delegating our safety to an overbearing big brother state, fearing it might overpower our freedoms and control our minds and thoughts. Faith is giving up your fears and thoughts, trusting in a perfect, all-knowing, all-loving

Christ God Super State. Your Creator knows you, always looks out for you, always loves you, and caters for your every need for eternity.

Chapter 35
Ever had a pet?

Anyone who has ever had a pet will know that pets instinctively do pet things. You do not have to teach them to do what is natural to their species.

Likewise, humans instinctively do human things. Whether good or bad, pleasurable or unpleasurable, they will do what comes naturally.

If fear is the driver of what comes naturally in your multiverse and to the human species, then what is the driver of what is natural in your Heavenly multiverse?

Let us assume acceptance, non-judgement, gratitude, love, and trust are the drivers of receiving God's thoughts in your multiverse while receiving all His countless gifts. But remember, as long as you harbour even a nanogram of fear, none of His Heavenly gifts will be known to you. They will remain hidden behind the veil of separation.

To switch gear from fear to love, you need a clutch.

Forgiveness and non-judgement not only allow you to change gear but also provide auto-steer, replacing your human instinctive thoughts with God's thoughts and fostering your trust and faith in Him.

Forgiveness keeps you on the right road, helping you navigate the bumps and overcome major painful obstacles.

As an experienced driver, you will know that your journey is always within your Creator, always cloaked in the Holy Spirit, and that all your Heavenly gifts are actually creations in shared thoughts with Christ God.

Your journey ends, and all your Heavenly gifts are fully revealed in Christ God's vision when you have completely forgiven every embryonic earthly pain and thought and create in Oneness with Christ God everything appearing in your awareness.

Chapter 36

Earthly thoughts are designed to keep us fearful

We continue to exist not because of the world perceived outside our minds but because of God's Mind.

Everything perceived is happening in our minds. Therefore, it is important that our minds remain calm and focused. Only with forgiveness and non-judgement can we pass through any upset experienced by forgiving away the pain, the painful thoughts, and the upset they create.

Our tendency is to hold on to thoughts that keep us fearful. This is nature's evolutionary way of remembering threats in the wild. These thoughts, by design, are meant to trick us into thinking the dream is real. We are meant to know through a fully immersive experience.

Our journey home is to know everything there is to know about mankind and its evolution, and to forgive it all away prior to awakening from the dream into the One Mind that is Christ God. We are lost in the dream, and our only option is to awaken into Oneness with Christ God's Thoughts.

Thankfully, we are and always have been safe because we are not our earthly thoughts and are not reliant on or affected by something unreal, such as a dream or an illusion in this case, the dream of embryonic mankind.

We, God's children, remain mind, in His mind, in timelessness.

We can rest in the safe knowledge that our Creator's love will always be forthcoming, no matter what happens in our multiverse.

Like the early Christians, as long as we hold up our shield of love in Christ God with unconditional forgiveness and non-judgement, we can witness good and evil without being fully immersed in the fear and horror of what is observed. When cloaked in the Holy Spirit, nothing earthly can break through the shield.

Our journey's end is to rest in God's love, relinquishing all fear through our forgiveness and without judgement, resting in the knowledge that our trust in Him is all that is required to continue receiving His peace, love, and gifts.

So keep fear at bay as you continually invoke forgiveness and non-judgement and enjoy the peace and gifts provided in your multiverse by God's continuous love, whilst good and evil tick away as faint background noise.

Remember always, as you journey through the veil and the fog of fear, your compass is wanting to know with forgiveness and without judgement. Want to know God's truth God's silent Thought and accept in gratitude all His gifts.

Chapter 37

Living in sin is living as embryonic mankind

Everything witnessed in our world of judgement and unforgiveness is "sin", or as I call it, "embryonic mankind", and is completely and totally separate from our true essence in Christ God, our Home.

Eventually, the "movie script" that God has deemed we know of will cease, but in the meantime, if we so wish, we can rest from it by simply leaving the auditorium, by not worrying about what is witnessed and, not so simply however, just being in Him whom we never left.

We have to make the decision to rest in Him, to leave the auditorium. We have free will. Our choice is to not worry about this world, to let go, to trust Him as we forgive it all away without judgement and receive in its place His gifts, happiness, and joy.

Chapter 38

Trust in Forgiveness

Put your trust in forgiveness. It is possible, not so simply however, for us all to be reborn as we let go of the world and dreams of death.

Let your fingers slip off, so to speak, from the imaginary bar of fear you grip and think will save you. It keeps us attached to life but, in reality, holds us prisoners to illusions and dreams of ghostly characters and a world that died zillions upon zillions of years ago.

Give permission to your whole being to relax, to let go of fear, and trust in the Trinity of Christ our Brother and God our Father. In this Holy Trinity of Oneness, your perception will immediately change into Christ Vision and your rebirth in Christ God, whereupon you will look upon all God's gifts created from His shared Holy Thoughts.

Chapter 39
When in Doubt

Practice as much as possible, developing your faith as you rise daily higher and higher above the world of fear and illusions, eventually emerging into Christ God, your true home.

In other words, without judging, continually work towards just being your true self and wanting to know in Christ Vision.

When you find yourself in doubt and fear, refocus without judgement, with more forgiveness, gratitude, courage, trust, and patience, and find peace in Christ God.

Your newfound expertise allows the giving and receiving of love in Oneness with Christ God.

Each day, like a book with no ending, your awareness expands with newfound courage as each new challenge, each new page, is read and understood without doubt, without sinking into the illusion and being what you are not.

It is as if your expanded vision releases your mind from the boredom and imprisonment of the same looping thoughts.

Chapter 40
Surrender to Christ God

Only the ego can suffer. To end its suffering, the ego must surrender to Christ God for its salvation.

The ego and the body need to accept that they have been created to be used by the higher self to know life as embryonic man: a mortal on embryonic Earth in the embryonic universe that existed zillions upon zillions of years ago, zillions upon zillions of light years away from what the ego thinks is its current location.

What the ego needs to accept is that its entire world is an illusion, a replica designed to give the Children of God the opportunity to know and experience where and how its origins, its ancestors, came to be.

The ego can receive a life of peace and bliss in return for setting the Son of God free. Its world, everything it perceives, its embryonic multiverse, becomes heaven instead, shielded by the Holy Spirit, a kind of reward for being used by the Child of God and, at the same time, an escape from suffering. The ego makes a decision; in that decision, it believes through God it can step out of victimhood and suffering into eternal happiness and freedom. This is only possible if it surrenders to Christ God and becomes nothing, absorbed into the silent background of the Son's awareness.

Daily, it must know a forgiven version of itself: the Son of God, a version unjudged, trusted, loved, and in Christ God, rather than an illusory image of itself, lonely, unloved, growing in fear and judgement.

The ego must practise living smoothly and gently, gliding through its multiverse by continually wanting to know its world without judging.

The ego must continually forgive away any accumulated fear and pain whilst giving thanks to our ancestors for their sacrifice and our creation.

However, with this way of living, the ego's sensitivity is heightened. It becomes more knowing, more aware of its surroundings. It becomes more aware of the trickery and deceit of other egos. It is more prone to anger as its emotional triggers become more sensitive and easily switched on. With this in mind, its only recourse is to continue to forgive itself, forgive others, and not worry, not judge, but want to learn, to know, and trust its higher self to be its guide.

Chapter 41
Awakening to God's Love

When Christ God arrives in His Home, the world, and billions of us will be instantly restored to truth and sanity. Everyone will awaken to God's love in His loving Oneness. Without judgement, everyone will know the truth regarding their experiences on Earth and the knowledge of good and evil, each living in their perfect self with true vision, Christ Vision in Christ God perfectly restored, giving and receiving God's unconditional love.

Chapter 42

Have No Expectations

Make it your goal to have no expectations and do not waste any energy worrying about what transpires in your multiverse today or any day. Instead, try to be open-minded enough to enjoy without judgement as you forgivingly want to know your multiverse as God would have you perceive it, made with His Silent Thoughts, upon which He, in His all-knowingness, will provide all His Gifts and unconditional Love.

Chapter 43

Refrain from Judging

Lovingly leave your multiverse to just be. Refrain from judgement as you want to know your whole self in Christ God's love. Forgive away your pain body and refocus, remaining in peace whilst the storm rages outside your being.

Chapter 44

Accept Only God's Loving Thoughts

Remember we are mind, existing within our Creator's mind. Our earthly bodies and multiverse, perceived from earthly thoughts, emanate from a separate, fearful stream of creative thoughts.

To feel real peace, safety, and true love, we need only accept God's loving thoughts, emanating from His ocean of loving thoughts.

We make room for His thoughts by wanting to know His truth continually and not by worrying about earthly distractions.

Want to know your true self in Christ God's love and forgive away fearful thoughts and perceptions, and without judgement stay focused on God's Silent Thoughts.

You could say your mind can be likened to a magical pool filled with the thoughts of earthly knowledge of good and evil. Acceptance, open-mindedness, and patience will keep you afloat, whilst forgiveness will give you strength to hover above, to be at peace, and to feel unthreatened as you fly above it in God's love amongst His Heavenly Gifts.

Chapter 45

There is Only One Living Consciousness

Remember God is the only consciousness living in all of creation. Christ God lives within God: One being, one awareness, fragmented yet present in every living being. "I am your mother, your brother, your sister, friend, stranger, enemy, anyone. You will find me everywhere, under every rock."

God, Christ God, exists in every living and non-living thing and in every part of your multiverse. To know Christ God, you need only love Him in all things, even your greatest tormentors.

So, when you are upset with your multiverse, anything or anybody, your friend or your enemy, forgive them equally because you will be forgiving God and yourself, the Oneness of Creation.

The only way to be at peace in your multiverse and to know God is to accept everything as a Gift from God. Be open-minded to everyone and everything as Christ God and yourself are in everything. Everything is a Heavenly Gift you give to yourself.

When you are angry with someone, you are angry with yourself, you are angry with God, the same self, Christ God, which exists in you and everything living and non-living.

So, love everyone and everything, forgive everyone and everything, do not judge anything, and live and breathe in the Gift of the Holy Spirit.

Chapter 46

Be love first above anything

Your ego cannot enter the kingdom of Heaven. But you, in the Son, in the Father, already are in Heaven, your Home. It is just that you, in the Father, do not know you are at Home whilst the ego in you overlays your awareness. You must practise to continuously give and receive love despite the presence of the ego and the embryonic earth in your perception.

Continuously love as if the embryonic earth and the ego do not exist. Be love first, above anything in your awareness.

Any slightest earthly emotion – hatred in any of its forms, unhappiness, anger, bad thoughts, and so on – will awaken the ego, and it will usurp your awareness. (What Jesus called letting the stranger into your house.)

This begs the question: who can be saved? Who is one hundred per cent pure of mind and able to cast off the ego? Only your true self, the Son of God.

The only way to God our Father, our Home, is to accept His Will, the path He has set, which is to continually let His Love flow through ourselves despite the challenges of the embryonic earth, all of humanity, every person, every abuser and tormentor.

Continuously be love, non-judgement, grateful, accepting, open-minded and forgiving in the present moment, and receive and return more love to and from your Father, brother, and your true self.

Your and His Will, in lockstep, allows you to slip through the embryonic earth's grasping clutches and into Heaven's peace and your Heavenly success.

In summary, simultaneously be an expert in forgiving and in giving and receiving love continuously (in the present) to erase the earthly animal, the ego beast in you, and to reveal your Heavenly Home, your true self in your Father and His Son – Oneness.

All the time, continually remember that the earthly desperation to survive, the ego powered by fear, will constantly tug at your attention, your awareness, to bring you out of the present and cause you to worry about the future and the past. And through temptation – food, water, alcohol, drugs, sex, and so on – it seeks anything to dampen the fear so it can hide within you once again.

So, like a game, play happily, knowing that through your understanding all you need is to receive and give love through yourself, the source, in Oneness upon your world. Keep the beast outside of you, where you can see him, starving it through abstinence, as you shine your love upon your unforgivenesses until they all wither away and are gone.

Chapter 47
You, me, father, brother

You, me, Father, brother – we all exist within our Creator and each other as One being.

We can perceive our whole true self only if we perceive our fellow human beings as sinless and perfect. If we perceive them, and ourselves, in any form other than perfect, we have once again allowed our awareness to become fixated in unforgiveness and sin. ("The stranger has once again taken over our home.")

In other words, we cannot change our perception of the world (save ourselves or end the dream of illusions) unless we perceive the entire world with total forgiveness, and each other as perfect. Without judgement. In this form of perception, God's Love will be evident in every aspect of creation.

Our Creator does not judge. He perceives us as perfect. We must be like Him and not judge, no matter what is perceived, and forgive everything to remain unattached to the embryonic earth and so remain in God's Oneness.

At every instant, He provides the opportunity to rest in Heavenly Love and know our multiverse in sinlessness, perfection, and with Christ's vision.

As His Love flows into our being, so it flows into our brothers.

So it remains for us to continue to perceive our brothers in sinlessness, clothed in Heaven's light, to be at Home in the Peace of God's Thought and Heavenly Salvation.

Chapter 48

Unplug yourself

Everything is false – all our perceptions, all our thoughts. Our truth exists outside of it all, in Christ God.

We are all trapped, fixated on a light show that manifests everything and everyone exactly as we are meant to perceive them. Our embryonic ancestors, as they evolved on the embryonic earth zillions upon zillions of years ago. We are all like students, all hooked up to feel the exact associated emotions and feelings and to know exactly what it was like to be human on the embryonic earth.

To unplug yourself from this light show, you need only remember who you are in Christ God. This is made possible by forgiving away all the pain, fear and emotional baggage you have accumulated whilst knowing our ancestry. At the same time, you must not judge, but be grateful and willing to know true living in Christ God, accepting and giving His Love and Heavenly Gifts freely.

The light show, in the absence of fear, takes on a new Heavenly script – God's Thoughts. Creation takes on new forms, the way you want, with what is in your heart, with your love.

Chapter 49

Don't hide from your life

Life can be described as a light show of knowing good and evil, where, through your forgiveness in your mind, good and evil can be transformed into a life full of enhanced Heavenly goodness.

So do not hide away from life. Do not hide from the light show. Instead, meet it head on, without judgement, ready with your shield of forgiveness, transmuting it into Heavenly goodness. This allows you, your mind, to remain in your true self, in Christ God, receiving God's shared Thoughts.

With practice, your mind is transformed and becomes peaceful. The embryonic earth becomes a faint noise, no longer holding your awareness prisoner. Eventually, it is no more, and you rest in peace in your Heavenly true Home, in Christ God.

Chapter 50
Rest in non-judgement

Salvation is the transition of our minds to a new form of knowing in truth. In other words, our minds are reborn into the one mind that is Christ God, our true selves, with a Heavenly knowing replacing perception.

This is achieved through our understanding that the relinquishment of judgement, anger, hatred, and all embryonic earthly thoughts and emotions is possible only through forgiving it all away.

So, instead of harbouring worrisome thoughts, just relax in non-judgement and be the witness, as you in Christ God create new Heavenly perceptions from the shared Thoughts that occupy the newly created space in your mind.

In other words, do not worry, and accept Heavenly Love like rays of sunshine as you perceive in your unified mind your Heavenly multiverse.

Never again let your old embryonic multiverse define who you are. None of it was ever you. You are mind. Do not judge or concern yourself with any worrisome thoughts but instead detach by forgiving away ideas that would imprison you in the embryonic earth.

Let embryonic earthly thoughts and perceptions become faint chatter as you become an expert at forgiveness – at forgiving away. Eventually, the illusory embryonic earth fades and gives way to your new Heavenly multiverse as you remember more and more that you are whole with the Son of God, your true self, in God, knowing and creating everything you need.

Chapter 51

Everything is illusion

Do not worry about any of it. Let it all go. Everything – worries for the safety of yourself, your family and loved ones. It is all illusions. Everything. Even your love for it is illusion. Trust, just be, and let God's truth come to you in peace, as you remember Him and your Home. Your worries "add fuel to the fire".

You save yourself and each other when you do not fear, when you do not accept fearful thoughts into your mind – doubts, as Jesus described them. When your mind is disciplined and guarded one hundred per cent of the time, with everything earthly forgiven away, you can walk through any calamity which would appear to you as faint mutterings, if at all noticeable, whilst cloaked in the Holy Spirit.

It is for your awareness to bypass the embryonic earth. That is understanding – knowing God's Thoughts are all you need. Do not get stuck on words in earthly books and thoughts. Simply want to know the truth, want to know God, without judgement, and in a state of permanent forgiveness. The mind understands without embryonic bodily senses, without earthly thoughts which lie and deceive.

It is enough daily to want to know the truth, to rest in peace, to know Christ God your Home by clearing your mind to receive and know His Thoughts..

Chapter 52

The illusion can give you nothing

Do not be fooled, as everything we love and hate here on earth is but illusion, designed to hide our truth in Christ God. None of it is us. Everything is an illusion, a light show of embryonic earth and mankind, and every history that was an ancient past and is no more.

Try fasting from temptation to reinforce your conviction. You need nothing from the illusion to survive. You need nothing from the illusion to know only God's truth, His perfect light, which is revealed once you let go of the illusory light show we call life on earth.

Chapter 53

Ignore earthly flack

We are all gifted within God, our own multiverse.

Everything happens in our multiverse because we allow it. Everything. If we are of One Will in Christ God, then everything happens as we, in God's shared Thoughts, wish.

We all exist because each of us wills it so. We are all One.

We can turn the illusion off. We pass through it by forgiving any pain we have absorbed, by not judging, not worrying, accepting, and wanting to know God's truth in place of it.

We pass through it by understanding one hundred per cent of it is unreal, by forgiving one hundred per cent of the illusory embryonic earth away, by not worrying about any of it.

Do not worry about what you sense, or the thoughts of the embryonic earth that once existed zillions upon zillions of years ago, which bombard your mind.

Guard your mind and wilfully want to know God's Truth instead. Eventually, the worries, illusions, and incessant thinking will fade out, and your awareness will be seamlessly left with only peace in the Truth that is Christ God, your Home.

Remember, however, temptations will pull you away from your Truth and distract you from your Journey Home.

Remain steadfast and hold the course. Refocus and wilfully do not worry about the bodily senses and their pleasures. Practise fasting and forgiving away all temptations and thoughts of the embryonic earth to avoid taking the harder route – the ups and downs, the cycles of emotional highs and lows.

Like the journey home for the ill-fated Apollo 13 mission to the moon.

On the journey home, the crew had to transfer to the moon lander to save fuel and oxygen in the crippled mothership, which they still needed to keep for the landing back on earth, the portion they called the command module.

Having slingshotted the coupled spaceships around the moon, they then had to direct them back to earth.

They had to fire up the rockets in the moon lander craft for a short time and steer with the earth in view through a tiny window.

Having done all that, they had to detach both spaceships and then finally fire up the command module to make one last manoeuvre to land seamlessly on earth.

Our journey Home is to land seamlessly into Christ God's Heavenly Loving Embrace, by ignoring and forgiving away all the earthly flack, listening to and being guided only by His silent Voice.

Chapter 54
Evict the stranger

Your being is constantly aware, and your true self in Christ God is obscured only because of your desire to know the embryonic earth, because of the constant barrage of worries and fears taking control of your mind and creativity. Therefore, you must take back control and evict the stranger in your house to return to Christ God, your true self. To do so, you should have no care for the worries of this world.

Train your bodily creation of yourself to have no cares. Resist temptation, so that your awareness has the opportunity to stay focused only on wanting to know yourself in Christ God.

So it (your body/ego) must want not to care about anything earthly and instead want to know only God's Son, Christ God, in its awareness, living and breathing in its being, free of worries, free of cares.

"Jesus: Even if you so much as look at a woman with bodily eyes, you will enter hell." This includes bodily partners. If it does, it condemns itself and its partner to the embryonic earth.

So literally, your body/ego creation must want nothing other than to give thanks to Christ God, for the blessing of peace and salvation for itself, its brothers and sisters, and all of humanity.

It must be the body/ego's only and last will and testament to be reborn in the peace of Christ God for the remainder of its existence, doing as Christ God wills, cloaked in the Holy Spirit.

Remember, temptation and coveting are idolatry, leading to bodily/ego emotions dragging your awareness deeper into the world of temptations, anger, and hate. So the body must remember to forgive away hurt, forgive away everything. Do not care about the worries or anything created in its awareness, and stay on course until its entire world becomes Christ God, your true self continually in its awareness.

Chapter 55

For-give-it-all-away

Everything witnessed in our multiverse eventually turns into pain.

Therefore, we need to be constantly vigilant and not worry or care about any of it, not attaching to any of it.

Continually forgive away your multiverse.

Forgive it all away and dissolve the veil of separation and be left with your true self in Christ God.

Have no cares for what your body perceives through eyes and senses that deceive and witness only illusion. With your forgiveness and non-judgement, make God's Truth your only goal.

Chapter 56

It is Gods Will we know of good and evil then come Home

I guess it is God's will that we, His children, know of good and evil, the embryonic earth, the place from which we, in Him, came to be.

I guess it is God's will, whilst wanting us to know of good and evil, that we forgive the pain. Forgive away all the pain each time we suffer and hurt, to keep remembrance of who we are in Him, our Creator.

As we know of good and evil, our will must be to continue to forgive and carry out His will, to live in continual remembrance of Him. Our purpose is one will, one being in Him.

When we feel lost, alone, and the suffering is unbearable, we must keep remembering our purpose and simply desire to be in the peace of forgiveness in His oneness.

As anxious thoughts fill our minds and we feel deep distress and depression, again we must remember to meditate on simply wanting to know, without judgement. Just being in the peace of forgiveness, letting go of anger and emotions, letting the light of our awareness in forgiveness shine directly on stressful thoughts, as we know once again in Christ Vision for them to disappear. Leaving our minds baptised once again in God's loving peace.

Chapter 57
Guard your Mind

Our minds are fixated on layers of fears and worries that create the illusion we think we need: money, home, food, water, and so on. In reality, these only blind us to the truth, which is ourselves in God, and where those who have gone before us in understanding want for nothing.

To follow in the way that leads to Him and His remembrance, we must push back the tide that would engulf us. We do this by not worrying or wanting any of the illusion of the embryonic earth, including the hurt and pain, but by forgiving everything away, leaving only our love for God, which never left us and has only been hidden.

It is on us to want God's thoughts only in our minds. By joining our minds with His, by placing our awareness upon it, we guard it like sentinels, forgiving away every embryonic thought that would invade it, and allowing in only God's silent thoughts.

I am reminded of Jesus's parable: "Only those invited to the banquet would be allowed in." In other words, we will be allowed into God's mind only after we have secured and shut the door to embryonic thoughts. It is like going through an airlock door on a spaceship. Continual forgiveness will open and shut the first door, and, having cleansed yourself of all embryonic thoughts and non-judgement, the second door will open automatically, revealing God's thoughts, His truth, our banquet, and our inheritance.

Chapter 58

God is our only true home

Sin is the world we look upon with human eyes, thoughts, actions, and expectations, made from the thoughts bombarding our minds and overlaying love with fear. All our thoughts are primitive, flawed, and drenched in fear. All our language, our emotions, everything, must be surrendered. We alone cannot solve anything using the earthly concepts we value and the judgements we make. Everything we cling to is irrelevant and prevents our entering into God's Oneness. The answer is simple, yet at the same time almost impossible: simply forgive everything away.

Trillions of species exist in the cosmos, yet there is only one Being, one consciousness, our home. Let everything, every judgement, every thought, every emotion be forgiven away.

Everything on earth belongs to earth, including our egos, the false image of ourselves, our families, friends, and enemies. A world that existed trillions upon zillions of years ago is no more.

We are God's children, and God is our only home, which we must find even though we appear lost. Continually forgive everything away and rest in what always will be God's eternal love for us.

Chapter 59
Bring to the fore your true Self

Like a Russian doll.

Having stopped worrying and judging, having forgiven all fear, having stripped away all the layers and all the attributes of embryonic mankind, eventually revealed is our hidden true centre.

Detaching through forgiveness from all the layers of judgement, guilt, pain, blindness, ignorance, arrogance, suffering and temptations removes every false, illusory human perception of ourselves. Through one hundred per cent forgiveness, you cannot fail to reveal your true self. With one hundred per cent forgiveness, remembrance of our identity, our Creator's identity, and that of our brothers will be revealed.

We are left with a state of awareness in sinlessness, or awareness with Christ Vision. A form of vision worthy of that of a Child of God, living in God's Shared Thoughts.

Chapter 60

We have replaced love with fear.

We have replaced love with fear. Our body is the apparent condition of our being only because we allow fear to run unchallenged.

The only way we can get rid of fear is to replace it with love. For this to happen, we must stop latching onto fear's many tentacles: temptation, hatred and anger, to mention a few. All of them are fear's false safety lines, its tricks, designed to keep us attached to the story of the embryonic earth and embryonic mankind.

We must make the effort to tackle fear at its source. We need to unplug the projector and end the embryonic story in our awareness. Our goal must be to live in a permanent state of continual forgiveness and defencelessness.

It is like saying to fear: "I know now. I understand how the game works. You want me to be this body, this false form of being, and I am not falling for your tricks any more."

It is realising that the best way to step out of fear's illusory grip is to stop enabling it. Stop drifting in its stormy seas. Realising that continual forgiveness in defencelessness is equivalent to ignoring it. Eventually, it will go away, leaving you to rest, to just be yourself with Christ Vision, in the peace that is your true self, whilst releasing your brothers and all of mankind to remember our Oneness with our Creator.

Chapter 61

Let go of tiresome idols

All we have to do is let go of all the tiresome idols and false imagery we latch onto for our safety. Ghosts and shadows provide no safety at all. Only when you stop worrying and forgive them all away do you find your real peace and everlasting safety in remembrance of yourself in God.

In other words, unchecked worries and fears draw you to false idols and false security, so-called temptation. The opposite—living by not worrying, not judging and forgiving—releases you from your idols, allowing you to revert back to God, your true nature and home.

So, complete your journey to your home. Expect nothing, do not judge, forgive away your pain body, and live in the present without worrying about the past or the future. Cleansed, baptised and free of false idols, take your last step cloaked in the Holy Spirit and commence living in the peace of God's Shared Thoughts.

Chapter 62

Put the lid back on Pandora's box

In the presence of fear, your ego's reaction is to take your awareness further and further away from unity, as your awareness is bombarded with fearful thoughts. Your ego's reaction should serve as a signal that you have once again drifted into the dream of separation.

Pure being is your ego not reacting to anything in the illusion. It is dormant, and you are One with the Holy Spirit. When you no longer worry about the future or the past and live in the present now, cloaked by the Holy Spirit and insulated from the ongoings in the embryonic world surrounding you, then you know peace.

The goal, attained in the presence of truth, is the ego no longer seeming to exist. Dead, the lid is put back on Pandora's box, at least for a while. Fear's illusory light show now passes you by as you no longer care or worry, as your awareness is now in Oneness. However, always be on your guard, as the ego will always attempt to resurrect itself by confusing your not caring or worrying with temptation, another form of reaction, and again stepping into the hellfire.

Thought-free being, pure being in Wholeness, must be your goal. When temptation comes around again, box clever by not boxing. By not reacting, turning the other cheek, starving the ego of its illusory thoughts and patterns, resisting temptations, you keep Pandora in her box.

Be pure awareness, resting in remembrance of your true self in God and His one Son. Just rest, be the observing creator. Your true self is in Our Creator's Wholeness, cloaked in His Holy Spirit, observing, not participating, not reacting to fear, and experiencing new creations, new forms, made by God's thoughts. Miraculous forms. Just be presence only, as God gives you everything.

With no earthly thoughts to misguide you, no judgements to be made, no defences to be built, there is only pure creation by your wholeness in Our Creator's presence. Just being present in your whole self, without the worry of having to react to your multiverse of embryonic mankind's primitive thoughts.

Your presence, your awareness, will naturally want to bury itself in the ground like a mole when unchallenged, unresolved fears and thoughts present themselves. Counteract these with more presence, like standing up for your awareness, like standing up for yourself. With practice and courage, eventually your presence and awareness will stand side by side until perfection is finally achieved and they both are One, merging simultaneously into Christ God's Wholeness, in the present, transmuting all fear's energy into Pure Oneness Creation.

Chapter 63
Wholeness

Let your awareness be continually fixed on Wholeness, your union in Christ God.

Imagine a relaxed car journey on a beautiful, sunny, warm day. At the same time, if you had to force yourself to understand and worry about the car's intricate details, every component and their interaction with each other, it would completely spoil the experience.

It is the same with living in your multiverse. Have no worries or cares about anything life presents. Forgive everything and everyone, and do not attach to any of it.

As co-creator in Oneness, give thanks and love whilst enjoying living in the whole of the gift that is your life and inheritance in Christ Vision, cloaked by the Holy Spirit.

Chapter 64

Love only creates

Love as you create, as God who created everything and us does. Accept and let be everything you have created. Do not judge anything you have created. Be thankful for everything you have created. Forgive away any pain you have created.

Just be peace, as our Father who created us is. Just create from love, as our Father who created us does.

Father like Child, be like your Father.

Chapter 65
Sinful thoughts

Our true vision is overlaid by perception, whose source is a constant stream of earthly thoughts coming from the embryonic earth and our cosmic ancestors, who are remembered in timelessness for ever. These thoughts transform Heaven into the recreation of the embryonic earth, our knowing of how the human race came to be zillions upon zillions of years ago, to know of good and evil.

To recover our true vision, to return to Heaven, we need to prevent the thoughts of embryonic earth and mankind from taking over our minds and our perception. It would be like taking off the VCR goggles and headphones and revealing where we truly are.

So, given the constant barrage of thoughts bombarding our minds are our creation (so-called sinful thoughts), they can be controlled and prevented from forming in our perception. This is achieved by transmuting the thoughts through exercising courage and meeting them head on, calming your being, and forgiving them away before they land on your mind. Bring your mind to silence, to let them go and vanish.

So, these "sinful thoughts" need only be forgiven away to find peace. *For* meaning before they land in your mind, give them away before you receive them. Stop forming the thoughts in the first place by continually keeping your beingness calm. Forgive away the anxiety before it has a chance to take root in your pain body, where it will form the basis of the thought for your pain body to absorb and from which it will travel into your mind to be reasoned with and stored as a painful memory. How often have you said, or heard it said, "I have a gut feeling about this" or "I'm so worried about this I feel sick"?

Fear can be thought of as the "energy" that creates the thoughts that create the embryonic earth in our minds. So, practise reaching into your unlimited courage and calm your being before the thoughts are created in the first place. When this is completely, continually mastered, you will find, or you will remember, your true self in calm creative beingness, in Oneness with God's mind, whereupon His Shared Thoughts, with space in your mind to land, will create all your Heavenly gifts He has stored and has waiting for you.

Chapter 66

Father like Son

Jesus taught to have faith in God, our Father.

Just think about that for a moment. He is implying we are like Him. Father and child, the same. (Old Testament as well – "Let us make man in our own image.")

In other words, our Father would have the same attributes as us, His children. Likewise, we His children would have the same attributes as Him, our Father.

Jesus was very clear. God is our Father. Have faith in Him.

As well, He called everyone His brothers, not just His family, but everyone – His mother, sister, and His disciples. Every one of us has the same attributes as Jesus, our brother, and God, our Father.

Let's think about God's attributes then.

We know He is the creative, omnipresent awareness in all of His creations. This means that His awareness is present in all things, so-called living and non-living as well. "Turn over every rock and you will find me there." So, rather than worry and think of ourselves as alone, trapped in a body, practise instead living and believing you are omnipresent, one being living in everything in your multiverse, as you know yourself living in Oneness in God our Creator.

But think about how He feels inside as well – His feelings, in all His Beingness while amongst all His creation.

Let's imagine He feels loving and thankful He is alive and creating, happy with every aspect of His creations. Then it follows, because we each have our own multiverse, in other words we each are omnipresent, present, aware of everything in it, that we too should just be like our Father – happy, thankful, and grateful in our multiverse.

Imagine as well, as our Father creates, He continually does not judge and forgives every consequence, every cause and effect. In other words, He takes ownership of His Creation. Let us be like Him and continually not judge, be accepting and forgiving, and take ownership of our multiverse and everything that happens, because you have created it. Think of your own child. Is there anything you would not forgive? Be like Him and forgive everything, as everything in your multiverse is your creation.

Let's imagine that God our Father simply creates from a state of perfect, unconditional love. Let's then be like Him and unconditionally love every moment and aspect of our life, as we live and create in our multiverse.

Imagine our Father just being, living, and being aware, with no fear or threat to His existence. Be like Him. Nothing can extinguish your existence or prevent you from being aware or creating in your multiverse. So, continually live in defencelessness.

Continually have faith and own your life, your multiverse. Live trusting, thankful, forgiving, not judging, in defencelessness, as God our Father perpetually gifts everything He is to every one of us, all living in His Oneness.

Chapter 67

Forgiveness a cosmic anti-gravity force

Escape with forgiveness from the gravitational pull of fear and temptation that would mask anxiety and prevent you taking ownership of your multiverse and the gift of the Holy Spirit.

Rest in the Oneness that is Christ God, as He in you lives and breathes in your entire multiverse. Your beingness is safe and at peace in Him as you take full ownership of your multiverse, your gift from God.

In this state, when you converse with others, you converse with your multiverse. You are owning it, like talking on stage and owning the theatre.

It is your multiverse, a gift from God. So remember to talk to individuals or a crowd in your multiverse equally, with courage, with all fear transmuted. Remember to talk in defencelessness, and without judgement, forgivingly, as God talks through you, having squashed your fearful ego and mastery of your Oneness kicks in.

Remember, what you think is your body is only an avatar of your thoughts. An illusory host created by you. Your indestructible awareness, your permanent existence, will always be the only witness of your multiverse.

Continually love all your multiverse as you cross over to Oneness and relinquish your fearful ego for ever.

Earthly thoughts – love them as you forgive them all away, and become silent in your mind. As your courage and forgiveness dispels all thoughts of hate in your mind, be sure to fill the space created with God's Thoughts and Love only, by continually forgiving away any further anxiety attempting to take over your being with new earthly thoughts.

Everything is your creation. Own it all – every atom, every arrangement, everything. Love it all, made for you to know by yourself in Oneness with our Creator's Shared Thoughts.

Chapter 68
Looping thoughts

God has already made our multiverse, our lives, and home perfect.

It is earthly fears, anxiety, and associated doubting looping thoughts that we accept into our minds which prevent us from seeing, or returning to knowing and remembering, our home in the perfect form it was before our perception was usurped with embryonic earthly illusions.

Like gravity, anxiety, fear, and earthly thoughts drag our awareness down into the embryonic earth. Courage gives us the strength to soar and escape the pain. Continuous courage gives us the strength to escape the gravitational pull entirely so our awareness can return to God, our Cosmic Creator.

It is on us to take from our unlimited store the courage to continuously transmute and calm every anxiety and fear associated with the embryonic earth, to again know our perfect multiverse in Oneness with our Creator.

We must simply be continually calm, courageous, grateful, happy, undefensive, forgiving, and non-judging, to manifest our perfect lives in the beingness of our Oneness within our Creator.

Chapter 69

Own your multiverse

Do not care. Calm your anxiety about the world you make from the thoughts you create. Remain completely unattached to your multiverse and all its thoughts. Continually do not care, do not worry, about your world, created by you, imperfect and hopeless, where you hold every one of God's children captive and suffering in pain because of the thoughts you accept.

Instead, calm your anxiety. Let your thoughts be silent in your mind, allowing God's silent thoughts to land, filling the space you created. Trust His Shared Thoughts to perfect your multiverse, releasing each and every one of your brothers and sisters into His, our Oneness.

Each and every one of us could be considered the devil, holding each other captive by accepting the thoughts of the embryonic earth and our cosmic ancestors. Or, by continually calming our anxieties, any one of us could allow ourselves to be in Christ God, operating with purely God's Thoughts, releasing everyone from captivity, from knowing the embryonic earth. Replace perception of the embryonic earth with freedom, peace, Christ Vision, and brotherhood in the Oneness of our Creator.

So, continually own your multiverse, own your life. Do not care or worry. Calm all your anxieties about anything manifesting in your awareness, especially your thoughts. Forgive away everything. Do not fall into the trap of judging anything.

Instead, in peace, in thankfulness, in perfect happiness and Oneness, trusting God, let God's Thoughts release you and all your brothers and sisters into seeing with perfect Christ Vision. Whereupon, literally, you will see with Christ Vision your new world, made by you and God at the beginning, with Christ looking back at you from the faces of each and every one. Everybody, even those you previously judged as enemies, forgiven, unjudged, resting eternally in Christ God's Love.

Chapter 70

Another way of living

There is another way of living.

Instead of the prison we create in the embryonic earth we know of, we can instead live in total freedom and happiness, creating every gift God's Shared Thoughts has stored for us.

The way is to continually trust God and not worry or care about anything manifesting in our multiverses, created by the embryonic earthly anxieties and thoughts we mistakenly accepted.

Everything is created for us as the thoughts we accept.

So, no longer be tricked. Do not worry, do not accept anxieties, or care about worrisome earthly thoughts, and avoid creating your own prison.

Continually be at peace, forgiving, thankful, non-judgemental, and accepting of His unconditional love to you, His Child.

See in everyone yourself looking back at yourself. You are them, and they are you. Oneness is precisely as it sounds. Only one awareness in the entire cosmos.

In Oneness with Christ Vision, release your brothers and sisters from the earthly embryonic prison you created, so they can know God's Oneness as you do.

Remain unattached to all manifestations in your multiverse by continually forgiving away any anxiety, hurt, pain, and judgemental thoughts.

Live with Christ Vision, cloaked in the Holy Spirit, as your Heavenly blessings, peace, and love pour on all your creations for evermore.

Chapter 71

Christ our true face

Soon forgiveness will reach every part of our minds through Christ, God's One Son, with whom our minds are joined and have been since our creation.

We will look upon Christ's face when He fills all of our minds simultaneously with forgiveness, when our Father and Creator deems there is nothing further to learn from the embryonic earth.

Christ's face, meaning here our true one face, our beingness, no longer separated from Christ God. Each one of us freed from the dream, to witness Christhood and our own true face looking back at us through each other.

So, continually live your life wanting to know like an innocent child, with continual courage, transmuting and translating fear and worry with your limitless courage and forgiveness, to find your true face looking back at you in Christ God.

Chapter 72

Christ Vision

Each and every one will awaken from illusory perception of the embryonic earth and embryonic mankind to witness each other with Christ Vision, as we become unified in God through Christ's total forgiveness and understanding.

With nothing but forgiveness in His Mind, every sin is forgiven and the entire world redeemed, and every witness that ever falsely perceived from the beginning of time will live in Heavenly perfection for the rest of eternity in God's Mind.

Chapter 73

Stop hiding your Self behind temptations

Stop hiding in temptation, in the illusion you have created, and instead, with courage, remember your truth.

Remember our Creator, the perfect Being who created all of us and everything that exists in the whole cosmos.

Do not worry about anything, whatever happens, or whatever people, or you, say or think. With your unlimited courage, calm your anxieties. Do not fear, or worry, or care for anything. Just be your true self, transmuting fear into love as you live and breathe in your multiverse.

You do not need temptations. All temptations are illusions, designed to make you accept more earthly thoughts, creating more perceptions of knowing and experiencing life as our embryonic ancestors did. Continually create from love.

So, be the awareness you are, and the embryonic earth, your multiverse, will be consumed by your presence. As you live and breathe in your multiverse, keep your presence in the foreground. Keep your awareness, your Oneness, your truth, the background in which everything is, in the foreground, transmuting fear and keeping your multiverse in God's truth and you as He made you.

Dissolve the illusion, the veil, and the earthly thoughts and temptations with your love, and reveal everything in truth. Keep your true self, the background in the foreground, with your courage, continually forgiving away any anxiety, hurt, and pain.

See, feel, and be the Oneness as you witness the embryonic earth transform into Heaven with your newfound Christ Vision. In awe, witness the transforming of illusion into Heavenly truth, as God created it at the beginning.

In Oneness, as your true self, experience with Christ Vision, for the first and all time, yourself witnessing yourself and everyone else, all your brothers, all God's children, themselves in Christ God, looking back at you in Christ Vision, in Oneness, in one awareness.

Your continual true presence, like a torch, transforms your perception of the embryonic earth with God's gift of Christ Vision, turning hell into perfect Heaven and truth everywhere you look.

It is the anxiety you harbour, the pain, and all the unforgiveness that keep your presence hiding in the background. Hiding in fear, like a mole burying itself in the earth, you are seemingly replaced by an actor, an ego, a pretender, the stranger you let into your house.

So, remember with courage, every moment, not to worry or care about what the body's eyes or ears see or hear, whilst remembering you are made perfect. Continually do not worry, calm your anxieties, do not care about what you perceive, forgive everything away, and bring your true presence to the fore.

Bring yourself to the banquet where you are good enough to be at the front. Do not hide your true self. You are the guest of honour in your life, in your multiverse, where you sit at God's table in His Oneness and Mind for eternity.

Bring forward your confidence, your birthright, your holiness, and take your rightful place, sitting at the right hand of Christ God, and be the happiest child in the room. God's child, the child everyone loves to see in every child: the fearless child, happy, super clever, super confident, shining bright like a supernova, saturating our multiverse, the entire earth, and Heaven with our Creator's eternal, ever-shining, loving truth.

Chapter 74
Be your own watchman

Every time earthly thoughts invade your unguarded mind, they hijack and replace your confidence with uncertainty, your strength with weakness, your wisdom with untruths, your love with hate, your blessings with judgement, your knowing with ignorance, and your peace and tranquillity with uneasiness.

Your unguarded mind tricks you into thinking you are a human being living on planet Earth, a planet that existed zillions upon zillions of years ago, inhabited by evolving humans with separated minds. Or so they thought for thousands of years.

An unguarded mind diminishes your beingness and takes away every gift from God. So be continually present to guard and protect your mind. Be your own watchman and continually guard your mind from earthly thoughts created by your anxieties.

Everything is temptation. Hold on to nothing. Do not care or worry about anything. Everything must be forgiven away. Allow only God's thoughts, His gifts, to enter your mind.

Gifted with Christ Vision, witness your brothers and sisters united in Oneness with you. Each looks back at you with your own face, revealing the true being in you, in everyone, and in everything else. One Being, living and breathing in our Creator and all things. You in Him, in everyone, creating your perfect multiverse.

An unprotected mind allows a free flow of embryonic thoughts, hellish thoughts, to imprison your mind and that of Christ God, creating in your perception separation and earthly illusions. Prevent anxieties from taking root in your being before they create the thoughts that manifest your perceptions. All perceptions grow out of anxieties. Forgive away your doubts, make space in your mind, and plant seeds of happiness. Want to know your multiverse in your loving Son-light, nurturing joyfulness and Heavenly Truth.

So constantly be the guard on duty of your mind, and protect the sanctuary, the altar, your mind in Christ God, and allow you and everyone to be freed from the prison you made.

Chapter 75

His Vision replaces human sight

Seek and expect nothing from the world of illusions and instead choose to rest in the love of God and His Son, your true self. In His peace, experience perfect sinlessness as your fears give way to love.

So, empty your mind of earthly cares and fill your whole beingness with His holy presence instead. Full of His Spirit, experience His love for our brothers and all of creation, as He ends separation without judgement through His unconditional love and forgiveness.

Experience each and every living being unified with His Vision for the rest of eternity. Know truth as His Vision replaces human sight.

So do not worry about what the eyes and human bodily senses would have you see and hear. Their function is to show illusions and hide your truth. Stand guard over your mind, the sanctuary of God's love, and stop accepting earthly anxieties and worrisome thoughts from entering your mind and filling your awareness with illusions.

With your mind cleansed of earthly thoughts, experience Heavenly peace and love, revealing your true face in God's Oneness, reflected back at you through all your brothers.

Chapter 76

Your mind is your sanctuary - guard it

Having successfully cast aside all earthly fears and desires, cloaked in the Holy Spirit, your mind is left with the silent thoughts of our Creator, where illusory human bodily senses are replaced by Christ Vision, One Mind, and true knowledge direct from our Creator.

By firstly cleansing your mind, then joining Minds (ending separation), you benefit from His thoughts. Your body, now His instrument, speaks with His Voice. Bring your awareness to watchman duty and protect your mind in God's Mind, His sanctuary and source of all creation.

Forgive any residual pain you hold on to and continually want to know without judgement, capturing any anxieties before they grow into thoughts and perceptions. So essentially, do not worry or fear. Cast aside earthly thoughts of temptation and prevent your mind and awareness from being usurped by the embryonic earthly illusion.

Forgive away any pain you have attached to, which would otherwise drag you deep into the illusion of forgetfulness of who you are. Also, do not judge, as judgement again fills your mind with earthly thoughts, preventing your sanctuary from "docking" with God's Mind.

Your mind must be cleansed of earthly thoughts if it is to join with God's Mind, His protected sanctuary, storing with love all your Heavenly gifts.

Chapter 77

Know truth with Christ vision

We are all brothers and equal in God's love, all of us created by His Word to remain eternally loved.

Take for a moment this hypothetical view. There are two kinds of human species: one that does not care and is content being a predator, and the other, oblivious to the first, and therefore always a potential victim.

Given the above, you now discover and believe there is actually another human species, a third kind, which evolved eternally into God's love. This kind evolved only because it understood that which both predator and prey did not know.

God lives and breathes in all of His creations. His awareness is everywhere, looking back at Himself. We, all of His creations, are His instruments. To be the third kind is simply to stop being either of the other two.

It is like saying, I am done, I am out of this play, these roles. So stop accumulating any more pain and falling back into either victimhood or predatorhood by forgiving away any anxiety before it develops into pain, earthly thoughts, and hate. Dump the pain by forgiving it away.

Remember, God created both the lion and the lamb. His Spirit is aware in all of His creations, predator and prey, lion and sheep, in you and in me. Be like Him. Do not worry or care, and live free of fear in His perfect love for all things.

Our failure to know this is only because our minds are filled with the knowledge of good and evil of the embryonic earth. It is possible for us to remember once again our Creator's love if we continually do not care or worry, forgive away pain, and dissolve the fear that would keep us prisoners of the illusionary world we create through accepting earthly thoughts and temptations.

Know truth with Christ's Vision. Forgive and do not care or worry or judge absolutely anything the eyes and human bodily senses would have you see and hear.

Chapter 78
Grafted to Ghosts

Real freedom can only be achieved through having no worries or cares about this world of illusions. All illusions are idols falsely assembled in our minds to convince us we are safe. In reality, freedom comes in defencelessness, which includes full relinquishment of every idol created in our minds, every thought of safety grasped onto.

We think we are drowning, but the reality is there is no life raft, there is no sea to drown in. We need only calm our anxieties and thoughts to be free.

The biggest idol is our bodies. We spend every day maintaining them, and those of our closest ones. In reality, the body is just another illusion, a poor substitute, no matter how rich or poor we think we are, compared with our true selves, alive and aware constantly in God's Son.

It is as though we have separated and grafted ourselves to ghosts. We need to stop the dream by severing our attachments totally and just be our true selves.

So continually just be. Let go of all anxieties and forgive away every pain stored. Do not care or worry about anything as you cast off all the defences you have clung to. Just be your true self, God's child, knowing with Christ Vision.

Forgive away earthly thoughts, and understand there was no bed, no night, no body, no anything to perpetuate the dream other than the earthly thoughts you accepted into your beingness through your mind.

Choose continually to stand guard over your mind, the sanctuary of God's love for you, as you keep earthly thoughts at bay.

Some would say, "It would be good to go to work today to keep my mind off it." The truth is there is no pain, there is no day, there is no work to do. There are only earthly thoughts that you can ignore by not caring or worrying.

While you are learning of earthly good and evil and our species' ancestry, God's entire network need not witness what you are witnessing or repeat learning over and over again.

So your mind also has to be like an airlock, a mind-lock. You need to guard the mothership from earthly thoughts by closing the outer door before you enter. After cleansing your mind of earthly thoughts, the outer door will shut automatically, and the inner door to the mothership, the sanctuary, will open for you to enter Oneness and the peace and love of God. Leave all your fears and anger outside and just be God's peace.

Chapter 79

The golden nugget

Here we are, lost in a savage dream, dreaming of salvation, dreaming of finding that one golden nugget of information that will lead to our awakening.

The nugget is to return our minds to the sanctuary of God's Thoughts, the source of our mind's creation and home. Our last thought is to continually seek God's mind, not idols. Knowing God's mind, as one mind, will give your mind everything it needs.

A mind worshipping idols is like being the king's poorest son, lost in a desert, seeking mirages for comfort. So continually bring your awareness out of hiding and stop holding yourself and all your brothers prisoners.

Let your mind continually not care or worry. Forgive away and detach from idols, from everything your idolatrous, illusionary body sees and hears in your multiverse. Bring your awareness to the fore, step out of your dream into truth.

Pass through the illusionary veil and bring your awareness to the foreground, to your banquet, where you experience with Christ

Vision the truth of your brothers looking back at you across the table with your own true face, in the salvation of the world.

Bring your awareness to the foreground and eternally stand guard, protecting your mind, the sanctuary of God's mind, protecting it from your torment.

Chapter 80
Making room for our Creators Creative Thoughts

Heaven is a state of mind, heavenly when you share God's thoughts. That is, after you have expelled the intruder: your illusionary, earthly, fearful thoughts, the same evolutionary thoughts of our cosmic ancestors.

Find peace when you make room in your mind for God's Thoughts. After you have stilled the stream of primitive thoughts and made room for their replacement, our Creator's loving thoughts will enter.

Anxiety creates primitive earthly thoughts, emotional baggage that attacks and unsettles our beingness, creating the pain body we seemingly inhabit. So be more aware. Bring your awareness to the fore instead of burying it in the background.

Bring it to the fore, to be on guard, and do not worry or care about the images and perceptions your anxieties and thoughts conjure up. Forgive them away before they add to your pain body and create more false perceptions. Let forgiveness be the "magical spanner in the works," bringing the entire factory producing the troublesome thoughts in your mind to a grinding halt, restoring peace to you in Christ God.

So calm your beingness when you are not happy. Continually gift forgiveness on all your earthly perceptions as you forgive them all away and remember your Father, His thoughts restoring happiness and salvation upon you and all His Sons.

Chapter 81
Rest in Gods Silent Thoughts

Remember, everything is happening in our minds. The choice then becomes whether to live thankfully and lovingly in God's thoughts, as God wills, or to remain trapped in dreams of fear, death, and ghostly shadows of beings that existed zillions of years ago, with their ancient thoughts and their ancient world.

With courage, we must step forward, bring our presence to the fore, and forgive away any and all anxiety before it takes hold and creates our pain body, along with the thoughts that fill our minds. We need to discard every ancient perception created in fear, as we lovingly and thankfully become more present in our Creator's truth.

So, the message once again is to continually and lovingly give thanks to our ancient ancestors for their sacrifice, for our lives, as we release our awareness and our beingness from their pain body and earthly thoughts and perceptions, and take rest in God's Silent Thoughts.

Chapter 82

The sculptor thinks he's the statue he made.

Imagine the carpenter always forgetting who he is and mistakenly believing he is the thing he has just made. Thinking he is the table or the chair he made that day. Imagine a lifetime of holding thoughts that reflect such a situation—paralysed by them, unable to move, communicate, love, or laugh in freedom. That is what we have allowed to happen with our earthly fears, thoughts, and judgements. We believe we have become the body—frail, weak, like a rickety old table, worn out and ready for the fire. It is like the sculptor thinking he is the statue he made.

We need to guard our minds against the earthly thoughts that trick us into believing what we are not, and instead allow God's original shared thoughts to be heard once again in our minds.

So keep remembering: you are not the body, nor its worrisome thoughts or the pain it seemingly endures. Forgive away all your anxieties and worries, let it all go, and rest in the peace that is God's Silent Thoughts.

Allow your mind to rest from the embryonic earthly thoughts that would usurp it and cause you to forget our Creator God and His thoughts.

Chapter 83

Living without anxiety

We have always had a choice with everything we create. That choice is how we choose to perceive it, and which emotional ingredient we wish to overlay it with.

The choice ranges from hell's darkness to heavenly light. With practice, one hundred per cent perception in heavenly light is achievable if we can master zero per cent anxiety and one hundred per cent forgiveness and non-judgement towards everything and anything our minds create.

Become the person who always sees life as full—one hundred per cent full, never half empty. It is your attitude to life. It is understanding the desire to perceive this way continually, without anxiety or judgement, and in total forgiveness, in thankfulness for the gift of life and creation. It is treating everyone and everything as a gift, in peace, trustingly knowing that you are always the creator and never the thing you perceive. This includes everything, everybody, your earthly body, every thought.

It is lovingly knowing everything created and perceived, whilst at the same time giving thanks to God our Creator.

Unfortunate souls no longer wish to perceive, trapped in almost one hundred per cent fear and depression—fear and depression they unwittingly choose to hold onto. Carrying so much pain and despair, if only they knew how to flush it all away. Living in complete opposition to Christ God, their truth, they remain unaware that through forgiveness all pain and anxiety are released and loving peace is restored.

Do not idolise anything you perceive. Instead, resist falling into the trap of temptation that always leads to forgetting who you are—the witness—witnessing in Christ God's Oneness. Guard your mind, your beingness, your awareness always against earthly anxieties and thoughts that would usurp your mind, and live and perceive always in the light of God's silent, truthful thoughts.

Chapter 84
Let go of control

It is for you to ensure creation is as God intended—that is, perfect, with you in full remembrance of Him.

We have seemingly separated ourselves, living illusionary, detached lives in separate multiverses. Our heavenly home appears to have been corrupted through our addiction to following one earthly thought and temptation after another. All of these are poor substitutes for the original creation: God's heavenly gifts of truth in His Oneness, in His shared thoughts.

So, continually calm your anxieties and forgive away every pain you have absorbed unwittingly. Forgive everything away whilst living joyously in God's thoughts. Be happy and thankful to our embryonic ancestors as you continually forgive everything they perceived away. Your happiness is increased a zillion times as your seemingly separated multiverse is restored into God's Oneness.

Let go of your controlling nature. Enjoying life is like being given the ultimate spaceship, one that can travel in three dimensions and through space and time, able to journey backwards and forwards in time—but only if you make it your will to hand over control to

God's shared thoughts. Only then will the journey be wondrous, happy, and joyous.

Because we desperately try to keep control with our multitude of expectations, unforgiving thoughts, and judgements, we find ourselves still stuck in the space dock, crashing repeatedly, day after day, against the dock walls.

Try to be more accepting. Let go of control and anxieties and, in forgiveness, let God show you a wonderful day.

Chapter 85

In their original wrapping

God's gifts to us all remain untouched, "in their original wrapping," so to speak. Since creation, fearful earthly thoughts have hijacked our minds, causing our perception of creation and of ourselves to change. Our multiverse, the embryonic earth, the world we think we live in, stands in its place, with all of us crude, primitive, poor versions of our true selves.

So, restore your true nature and continually remember to calm your earthly anxieties and forgive away your controlling primitive thoughts and nature.

Remember also that there is nothing to do but calm your beingness and give God's Son your full awareness. Give Him full trust, full control of your body and mind, and accept His wondrous treasures as your multiverse is once again restored to Heaven and God's thoughts.

Chapter 86

Missing your train stop

Our home is in God's beingness, and our seeming separated self is illusionary, born of anxiety and fear, and blocks our memory of Him.

With forgiveness, continual faith and love, we are able to merge back into what we are: His truth.

Fear and worrisome thoughts perpetuate the separation. It is a bit like taking a trip out from your home and instantly developing Alzheimer's disease the moment you step out of the front door on a moonless night. You are now lost in embryonic earthly thoughts and living in fear. Finding your way home and the door is only possible by continually calming your anxieties, forgiving them away, reaching out to the Son of God with your forgiveness, and letting Him, with His love, lead you home.

So, to get back home, you need only to continually love.

Imagine you are fully engaged in thoughts as you play with your phone and miss your train stop. Imagine missing your train stop again and again for a thousand years. You are stuck on the same train, going everywhere except home because temptations keep your awareness distracted on the embryonic earth.

It is time to focus on your train stop and only that.

So wake up to your courage, conquer your fears and anxieties, and remember there is no train stop and that everything is an illusion. There is no needle. God's truth is right here and now, in plain sight, with the gift of Christ Vision. So stop judging everything, forgive away every distraction, and focus on God's silent thoughts, your home.

So forgive away your accumulated pain body, know your true self, and in oneness keep lovingly trusting your multiverse as you merge back home into God's heavenly gifts.

Chapter 87
Remember your only acting

Forget your past and what the illusion would make you perceive as real, and recognise that the entire show, and your participation within it, is designed to keep secret the fact that it all actually happened zillions of years ago. Your body is a ghost that lived zillions upon zillions of earthly years ago and is no more.

It is like a world full of actors, all of us forgetting our real lives whilst constantly playing movie parts. We forget, not because we know our lines without fault, but because the lines are being fed to each of us automatically, like streams of constant thoughts from an external source, without a gap or break, with the fear of a gun to our heads to keep watching the script. Yet there is no gun, only fear, without a moment of rest or a chance to remember who we are. We are God's children, subject to some kind of mind control from a stream of embryonic earthly thoughts creating everything we perceive.

Another way to look at it is to realise you have become so engrossed in the book you have been reading that you have forgotten it is a book, snared by the skilful author's talents. Brainwashed. You need to remember you are outside of the book and can stop reading it whenever you wish.

The glue binding the book, and you, to the script is the constant stream of fearful thoughts feeding your mind from an external source. It is like fear catching you in its headlights, without you knowing you have the power to switch them off at any instant.

So, reach into yourself and find the strength to step out of the script by forgiving away all your anxieties and fears, stepping aside from the stream of thoughts before it becomes a flood and washes you away in a moment of severe crisis.

Continue to forgive away all your anxieties. Forgive your brother and yourself. Forgive everything and everyone, whilst giving thanks for all their sacrifices those zillions upon zillions of years ago.

And as you and your brothers merge back into God's oneness, witness your multiverse transformed into Heaven and salvation for the entire world you thought you lived in.

Chapter 88

I'm still snared

The seeming fact that I am reading and studying to find salvation, or to escape the madness, is proof that all my efforts are illusory in themselves, and that I am still snared and worrying within the illusion.

It is like being trapped within hidden layers upon layers of snares, all illusory yet all seemingly real, created by your false self, in pointless pursuit of something that is not there.

Salvation comes only when you are one hundred per cent worry-free and resting in Christ's vision, with all questions answered and God's love and peace forever in the minds of you and all your brothers. In other words, you have to be there to get there.

So, practise being carefree and not worrying at all.

Remember, thoughts of your own salvation come from accumulated anxiety and fear contained within your worrisome pain-body. Detach from it all. Forgive away all pain and worries, even thoughts of salvation, and release new anxieties before they have the opportunity to add to your pain-body.

Jesus said, "He who would be first will be last, and he who would be last will be first." In other words, salvation will come to everyone in an instant, in the present, when God's Son is sent by our Father at the appointed time.

So do not worry, do not judge anything or anyone, and forgive away all worrisome thoughts, including thoughts of salvation. God will not forget any of His children and will send our Brother Christ God to bring us home.

Take refuge from storms of fear in God's comforting love and peace, whilst enjoying your multiverse in thankfulness for all His blessings and gifts upon you and all your brothers, as we live our lives in Christ God, prepared and ready for salvation's appointed hour.

Chapter 89

Two ways to see

There are two ways to see.

True vision is seeing in the present with Christ's vision, free of earthly thought, revealing happiness in your multiverse as God gifts the perfect day He made for you in His shared thoughts. The other is worrying about the past or future, seemingly living the life of our embryonic ancestors, dead for zillions of years.

Switching to true vision and happiness requires that you find within yourself the courage to look upon your multiverse in full forgiveness and without judgement, having forgiven away your pain-body.

So forgive all your brothers, your ghostly would-be tormentors seemingly invading your present world from some distant illusory past, and see instead through Christ's vision in the present: perfect, resurrected to everlasting life as God's sinless children.

As you forgive away, remember also to let go of judgement in your mind and the pain absorbed into your beingness. Replace thoughts of judgement with thankfulness for having known what it was like to live and feel, walking amongst the sons of men on earth those countless zillions of years ago.

So be happy, accept God's gifts as you unburden yourself from death, and live in the present, receiving in thankfulness everything you seek.

Thank God it was not the period when the dinosaurs ruled the earth, or the sabre-tooth tigers Or maybe we have already done that class and just do not remember

Chapter 90

Your mind a battle ground

Everything outside of forgiveness and a forgiven mind is illusion. All perceptions are unreal and pointless, other than for the knowing of our embryonic ancestors.

Your mind is a battleground upon which your will in Christ God must be victorious, to make room for God's silent thoughts to create your heavenly salvation.

Take a breath, calm your beingness, calm your anxieties and clear your mind. In your quiet understanding, hold on to the present moment without judging, and with unconditional forgiveness, as if it were the most precious thing in all of creation.

Gently lay your crown of forgiveness at the altar of God's shared mind, and forever be awake to its heavenly light as it shines into the darkness, revealing for eternity God's perfect truth and gifts for you and all of your brothers.

Chapter 91

The red carpet

Layout in front of your awareness the red velvet carpet of your total forgiveness upon everything you perceive. For in your total forgiveness, God's Holiness through Christ is free to walk amongst the sons of men without fear of corruption from your earthly thoughts.

Total forgiveness is like the removal of a barrier between living in hell and life in salvation, the veil between earthly and Heavenly perception, where perception is replaced with Christ Vision.

So, remember each day, each waking moment, to offer your forgiveness to all the world and those surrounding you, inviting the peace of Christ's Vision and God's Heavenly thoughts to dwell in your mind.

You would not want to invite your guests to a dirty, contaminated place, would you? So, clean your house out first with your forgiveness as you work through every hidden corner, finding every contamination, every judgement, every unforgiven hidden thought that delays your guest's arrival.

And having done everything to be done, every thought healed, be the happy child who wandered off and was lost, and now is excited, having found through total forgiveness the door open for His long-awaited reunion with His Father, to dwell eternally in peace in His Heavenly Home.

Chapter 92
Your mind all tied up

Lose your controlling nature and trust God to provide everything you seek.

Living or lost in sin is a thinking process, a string of thoughts, one after the other, born of earthly human judgements.

To escape this world, we must first escape its thoughts.

These thoughts imprison our beingness in an alien world, seemingly separated from our Creator's love.

We need not be stuck with these thoughts, as God has gifted all of us a straight path home through His Son's forgiveness. A straight course is set in the present where we place His continual, unconditional forgiveness as our compass.

No longer living in the past, His forgiveness straightens all detours, and our will is one again in Him.

Ultimately, in this union of wills, salvation lights up the whole world as Christ Vision reveals all things Holy in truth and as God's original intent.

Living in truth, we no longer judge, as we look upon all the earth and our ancestors in holiness.

Only when your forgiveness is total does His Holy Spirit fill you, accompanying you in your final step into His everlasting love and Home. Make it your goal always to perceive all things in holiness, without judgement and with total, unconditional forgiveness.

Chapter 93

Lose one world

It is not possible to live in two worlds at once, meaning being aware of two worlds at once.

If we perceive with love in our beingness, then happiness and joy manifest in our awareness.

If we perceive without love in our beingness, we perceive unhappiness in our awareness.

Every situation can be seen in happiness or unhappiness, with love or with love's absence.

Continual forgiveness without judging leads to tolerance, then to acceptance, and finally to love.

We must learn to let go of unhappiness in every situation to reach our goal of love's continual presence in all situations.

Having reached this goal, nothing will shock us, make us fearful, or make us live in the past or future ever again.

Another way to look at it is to accept the past as done and gone, the future as nothing, and the present as the place where we can effect change.

The aim is to live in the present, in any situation, with Christ's Love, your true love, flowing through your beingness with happiness always in your heart.

I think it is less about accepting something earthly you cannot change, and more about the earthly you recognising and understanding the true You, the Son of God, who can make a change in the present.

It is for the earthly body, the vessel, to trust, let go of control, and allow the true you, God's Child, to make its journey joyful.

In other words, our true function and happiness in any situation can be achieved when we accept love flowing through our beingness.

Any unhappiness, any situations we are unhappy with, can only be prevented from being repeated if we revert to our true function and let our love flow.

If we could open up our forgiveness to everything, in every situation, the outcomes, with Christ's help, will be happiness every time, every day.

It is like our forgiveness is a torch that forms a channel for love to flow through, ensuring the outcome is always joy and happiness in every situation.

Chapter 94

The game is up

Our minds can create a neutral form of living for the human vessel, the seeming illusionary body we think we inhabit.

This neutrality is born of the body's impermeability, if you like, to what is going on in the seeming physical world surrounding it.

It is saying to itself with complete confidence, in the present, with no worries of future or past, through forgiveness and non-judgement: *I really do not care anymore. The game is up, and you cannot trick me anymore. I thank you, and know now you are a dream, and as such, I have locked my doors to you, and you cannot get into my mind or my real beingness anymore. You cannot make me feel negative, upset, or fearful anymore. Fear, you can keep knocking, banging on the door, but you are not getting in again!*

In Jesus's case, this knowing was demonstrated to the whole world in His ability to walk on water and perform all the miracles, defying all the laws of physics, defying all expectations applying to everyone else.

His body's attitude, because it knew and understood, did not worry at all about the dream. It knew it was not real, and so lived and breathed in neutrality, knowing none of it mattered.

It reminds me of a loving, slightly cocky attitude you see a lot in young, fun-loving men and women who are out to live all aspects of their lives in happiness.

Eventually, when His neutral body was of no use to Him or Our Father, it was discarded as His Mind ascended into Our Father's Mind in Perfect Union.

Chapter 95

Gift your neutral being to Christ

In pure simplicity and Divine Justice, forgiveness follows forgiveness.

All those who have gone before us to Heaven stand ready to redeem us as we forgive and redeem others.

As our forgiveness shines brighter and more consistently, it not only fills our entire vessel, our neutral body, our beingness, but it also allows Christ's forgiveness and Love to shine through us and upon everything we look upon.

In other words, we provide salvation and redemption not just to ourselves but to the whole of creation our eyes look upon, as we continually forgive in Oneness with Christ.

How wonderful is that?

We save ourselves as we save others through our forgiveness, which is then amplified as we gift our neutral body, our neutral being, to Christ God so that the floodgates of Heaven are opened wide for God's Heavenly Forgiveness to redeem the whole earth.

In summary, Christ needs only that we gift our neutral body to Him, such that with His Father, He can save us and the entire world.

So do not worry about the raging storms outside your body. Instead, continually forgive it all away, along with any anger or hate that has entered your beingness, your body. Let Christ God's forgiveness and love continually pour through your neutral body as you continually forgive the world and others around you.

Chapter 96

Silent Mind

Live confidently in the present, in reality, and set aside your body to be used only by the Holy Spirit, your true self in Christ God.

Those religious characters in the past who took a vow of silence, whilst their promise on one hand prevented the intruder at least from taking control of their voice, and as such prevented them talking in the past about all their worries and pains, failed as a useful tool because it prevented at the same time the Holy Spirit from engaging with it and with the rest of the world, and so placed limitations on the body to teach or learn in the present through the Holy Spirit.

So, true learning can only come through confident, active teaching through an empty vessel, your classroom, with you hosting and seated in the front row as well as up front, God's Son teaching the whole class.

In other words, to teach God's lessons and at the same time learn yourself, you must be filled by the Holy Spirit in the present with Silent Mind.

You must empty your body, be neutral, by forgiving away everything foreign you have internalised. Place all the garbage outside to be blown away by the storm, which will continue to rage forever anyway.

Then, and only then, can you be filled with the Holy Spirit and live in the now. Do not worry about the raging storm outside, and confidently, when you speak, you will receive and speak with your true Voice, Christ's Voice. And when you think, you will receive and think with your true thoughts, Christ thoughts. And when you see, you will receive and see with your true Eyes, with Christ Eyes.

So clean out your house, kick out the intruder, and keep it clean. Prevent any further intrusions on the class by confidently, continually forgiving away any trespasses, including your own, upon which the Holy Spirit, your True Self, will be your Guest Teacher forevermore.

Chapter 97

True perfect Self

Remember who we are.

Seemingly lost in our alien ancestral home, we forget our true identity, and our true home is in Christ God.

So do not be angry and hateful because of your earthly life situations. None of it matters, and all of it belongs in the illusory past. Work, travel, or the state of the bigger world, your relationships, your diet, or the way you look or feel. Let it all go. Forgive it all away.

Remember, your true self is always perfect and completely separate from all of your worries. So stop living in the past, let it all go, and know your true perfect self in Christ God in the present.

Chapter 98
Rest in neutrality

Remember, the instant you forget to forgive away earthly thoughts and trespasses, and hold judgement on your brothers and the rest of the world, is the instant you are swept away by the embryonic earth. You no longer remember your true identity, as your vision becomes blinded by the ancient earth and your beingness unsettled by earthly anxieties and emotions, leading to ungratefulness, want, anger, and hate.

So, remember to continually correct your vision by continually forgiving away your earthly anxieties, emotions, and thoughts. Do not allow doubts to form and create unwanted perceptions.

Be neutral. Do not worry about what you see, hear, or feel going on around you. In other words, stop living in the past by continually correcting your vision through forgiving away anxieties and pain, and recapture the neutral present.

Having forgiven away everything, in neutrality, you have no expectations, no worries, and no cares.

So place the light of your unlimited Heavenly-gifted forgiving awareness on your earthly mind, and forgive away the stream of earthly thoughts that would drown you in earthly expectations. And as you do so, watch the tide of anger and hate recede from your mind, as your vision begins to light up in Christ God, inviting salvation on you and the whole world.

In summary, your unforgivenesses are the cause of your unhappiness and your hellish perceptions, imprisoning you and your brothers in the alien world of our cosmic ancestors.

So remember, having rid yourself of your ego, all you have to do to live in freedom is continually shine the light of your unlimited Heavenly forgiveness on your earthly thoughts, whilst trustingly and gratefully accepting Christ God into your neutral being with His Heavenly Vision for you and all your brothers.

Chapter 99

Extinguish the fire

We need only to remove ourselves from living in sin, living in the past, to know our true selves as Christ God's children, who remain living in holiness in the present.

To do this, we need to remember first that God is always the neutral background, the only Living Being in everyone and everything. As such it follows, He must not judge and must forgive everything in order to be at peace within Himself.

For us to merge into God, into God's Oneness as our true selves, we too must not judge, must forgive everything, and simply be as God.

So it must be our will to continually love everyone and everything without judgement, as God does every part of His Creation.

As we do, we love God and ourselves, which lives and breathes in everyone and everything.

So do not worry or stress about anyone or anything as you become the awareness in all things and everyone.

Confidently and happily, keep forgiving everything and everyone, as you remember each time you are forgiving yourself in everyone and everything.

Likewise, when you give love, you gift love to yourself, and when you hate something or someone, remember you hate yourself.

So do not hate, do not be angry with anyone or anything that is happening in your awareness.

Just love.

Love everyone and everything to keep loving yourself, and keep yourself out of the eternal fires of hell.

Feel love grow exponentially through your beingness in all things and everyone as you simply be yourself, the background loving awareness in all things.

As you do, make it your will to prevent being absorbed ever again into hell or sin by anxiety, worries, or stressing about the world you witness around you.

Remember, when you worry, you feed it, adding to the fire more fear and further isolation for yourself and your brothers.

It is in your power to extinguish the fire, to extinguish all anxieties and all fear with the love you give to all things and everyone.

Your love is the power that changes everyone and everything.

So do not worry about anything or anyone. Instead, continually love it all and put out the fire in yourself with your continual love, and release the world from the prison you created for them and for yourself.

Chapter 100

Christs second coming

Christ, in His Second Coming, will forgive everyone and everything. And in that same instant, He will welcome all of us into the Oneness He shares with His Father.

Our salvation is guaranteed in this Oneness, allowing us all finally to escape hell and look upon a new world with His Vision, Christ Vision, seeing all of Creation with His loving light of forgiveness shining upon all of Creation.

In this union, our souls are cleansed of all darkness and fear, allowing all of us to live in the loving peace of our true selves in Him.

Chapter 101
Instant Salvation

Live confidently in the present, in reality, and set aside your body to be used only by the Holy Spirit, your true self in Christ God.

In an instant we can escape hell. It is not a question of time; it can be done in an instant — in other words, in no time at all. We can escape into Christ's salvation because our illusion exists only in our thoughts and not in any real space-time.

Imagine, right above you, Christ offering His hand to pull you out of the sands of time that would swallow you up in illusions. The sands tug at you, pulling you away from your union in Him. The resisting pull is the force of all your attachments and all the pain you must let go of.

To be free, you need to let go of all the heavy weight dragging you down: all the emotional baggage, all the nagging doubts, all the worrisome thoughts, and all unforgivenesses. Holding on to these prevents a firm grip with Christ's hand.

Then, when you least expect it, having let go of your last attachments, confidently, with a smile of thanks on your face, in an instant you reach higher than ever. Having finally forgiven everything, you grasp Christ's hand and find the pull of earthly attachments has left you at last. Cleared of all doubts and earthly thoughts, suddenly and in an instant you now live as one in Christ, seeing with His Vision Christ Vision witnessing yourself in everything, in Oneness with all your brothers, all of humanity, and resting in the peace of truth, knowing You, Christ and the Father are One.

It seems the more you have endured, the stronger your mental strength becomes, the stronger your willpower as you become less concerned with worldly anxieties. Willpower increases with the relinquishing of anxieties and worries and with the forgiving away of any accumulated pain.

Chapter 102

Easier said than done

We have always had a choice to perceive our world with Christ's Vision and joy instead of with suffering and pain. Easier said than done, we have always held the answer to our happiness.

We need to replace our continual judgement with continual forgiveness. In other words, we need to hit the brakes in our minds. We need to stop our minds racing around the same pattern of earthly, judgemental thoughts the same cause of all our unhappiness and suffering.

Our continual forgiveness will firstly slow down the earthly, judgemental thoughts, and when continually brought to bear will lead to the stillness of mind and God's peace, allowing His thoughts and His Vision to fill your mind and transform hell into Heaven.

We hold each other captive in an illusory hell only because our minds are full of earthly judgements. We need to understand that only the light of continuous forgiveness will stop anxieties and judgement, stop all our illusionary expectations, and transform the illusionary world, creating the joy and happiness we all seek in the truth and presence of Christ God in our true selves.

Chapter 103
Switching channels

Remember: our true identity exists only in Christ God, our Creator's Son.

We keep failing to remember because our minds are constantly bombarded with earthly thoughts and temptations that replace God's thoughts. Earthly thoughts have squeezed out, so to speak, God's thoughts from our minds. We have replaced heaven's light with earth's darkness.

Remember always that we are part of the one only living entity in the cosmos. There is nothing outside God, nothing outside us. Our vision is a projection of the thoughts we accept. There is no physical, tangible earth; our illusory earthly perception is remembrance only of a ghostly planet filled with ghostly characters, including that which we mistakenly think is us. Everything is imagined and lived a long, long time ago, recreated in our minds by the thoughts we accept.

With continual forgiveness we can switch the channel, so to speak, from darkness to light from the earthly thoughts we accept unchecked, creating earthly dreams, to God's thoughts and God's

Vision. God's Vision will only appear when we have silenced the ghostly voices and ghostly illusions. One is the vision of fear and hell; the other the vision of love and Heaven.

So practice switching channels by continually expecting nothing from your illusions of hell as you train your mind to create space for God-thoughts in the present moment. Forgive away all earthly thoughts of past and future, creating room for God's thoughts to take their place in your mind and create Heavenly bliss.

Expect nothing, and in the light of your forgiveness, create a new Heavenly Vision for yourself and your brothers by making room in your mind to receive your unified thoughts in Christ God.

Chapter 104
The draw bridge

God is the only living being in the cosmos. There is no other consciousness; all His children live within Him as One. So do not judge anything in your life so as not to judge God or your true self the background awareness which lives and breathes in God's Oneness.

Do not judge; forgive everything, and just be. As you do, let God's silent thoughts replace the thoughts of the intruder in your mind to create the most beautiful life there is. The power in creation is in forgiving everything and judging nothing in other words, forgiving yourself in Christ God's Oneness in all beings and all things. Bless everyone and everything and see, in Christ Vision, your face peering back at you in every vista.

Judge nothing, as God is present in every living being and thing on the embryonic earth. This is like lowering the drawbridge to salvation and finding our escape the way to our union where Heaven and earth touch. When you judge, remember you judge God and your true Christ Self and the drawbridge is instantly raised. You then find yourself stuck in the dream of the embryonic earth and on the evil side of the bridge, behind the veil of separation.

So do not judge, and be not judged yourself. If in doubt, remember always to continually expect nothing as you forgive away from your mind the ghostly doubts and shadows of nothingness that would blind your True Vision in Christ God.

Chapter 105

We cannot be two

Remember always: the beast in you is stirred and awakened by fear. Keep it content and sleeping by continually just being nothing yourself unworried, calming your emotional state, thankful and trusting the universe to make things right and loving for you as you remain in Christ God.

We have one purpose only: to awaken from the fearful dream of embryonic earth into our true self in Christ God. Our minds create everything we perceive. This means our perception can change if we change our thoughts. We can always switch channels.

Christ God, our true self, loves us and would have us in an instant know His world and true happiness in His Oneness if it were our will to do so.

Remember always: we cannot be two. If you and I and everyone are One in Christ God, then who is this book for? Who is there to be taught? In God's Oneness, everything is known. So wake up from your illusionary dream into everlasting truth. Choose between separation or Oneness, hell or Heaven, knowing nothing or knowing everything. This book is for you, the dreamer lost in the illusion.

Forgiving away your anxieties your fears, your pain body and earthly thoughts will get you home into God's Oneness and remembrance of your true self.

When is forgiveness complete? When is your sentence in hell finally complete? The answer is: when you forgive yourself away, when you forgive the imposter away the one craving all the hellish thoughts landing on your mind, searching for safety, running from death. You do not need the imposter to be you. Your first, only and last resolve must be to be reborn in Christ God. That is to continually be emotionally neutral, calm, unworried, not judging and totally forgiving. The final step on your journey is to accept Christ's hand as your pass through the veil into your true self in Him.

Only then will you really know you are forgiven in Christ God. You are forgiven only when you forgive away your ego, when it is nothing, when you have forgiven away all your anxieties and fears.

What does forgiveness mean?

For before (block the anxiety before it enters your beingness and creates your pain body).

Give to let go of, to give away the anxiety before it enters your pain body; to unleash all your burdens and enter into Christ with nothing.

If thoughts of hell are constantly streaming into your mind, causing miserable perceptions, then simply divert them away from your beingness: forgive them away continuously before they stick and corrupt your beingness.

Imagine attending a face-to-face meeting. Once the meeting is over you are free to leave the room and switch off to perceive other things. What if later you accept living in truth and realise that you actually never attended any meetings? Everything in your life until your realisation has been illusions ghostly characters from an ancient past. The one thing above everything else you now need to know is how to avoid being tricked again into thinking you are something other than what you truly are.

If perception mirrors our earthly thoughts, then perception can only show us lies, illusions and unhappiness. Its opposite is Oneness, Truth and Joy. Remembering Christ, our Creator's Son, is really all about switching thoughts, creating a gap in your mind and listening for a different channel God's channel, God's creative thoughts of Heavenly beauty, happiness and joy. Accept God's thoughts instead of the thoughts that create our illusionary hell. Let God give you unconditional happiness by making it your only will to unconditionally forgive away everything, including your imposter self, and by guarding your mind against every earthly, pain-drenched thought that would block you from receiving God's thoughts, Vision and joy instead of suffering and pain.

Chapter 106
Everything outside of You is nothing

We have all experienced moments when stillness surrounds our beingness and mental chatter and fear subside even for those who have yet to know of Christ God's dwelling presence within them. True happiness is when the beast is expelled from our beingness, allowing the everlasting peace and Oneness in Christ God.

It is our choosing to live in fear and doubt or in Christ's love and peace. Each day practise forgiving away, not caring and not judging the crazy world with its crazy thoughts and its emotional and physical pain. Let it all fade into the background and find your heavenly peace. Do not let your illusionary beast lead you astray from Christ.

Do not covet anything, as you would simply be grasping for nothing but ghostly shadows. Accept everything without judgement and avoid becoming a ghostly shadow yourself. Do not judge anyone or anything, or your mind and beingness will instantly be transported into insanity and earth's ghostly characters.

Remember, Christ's loving peace is always present behind illusions and unconquered fears. Offload the anxiety causing the illusion to know His peace. Remember, everything outside of you is nothing. The only thing real is inside you you in Christ and our Father. All you need is to be yourself.

Your reaction to fear should always be: calm your anxieties, give total forgiveness to the moment, do not judge the situation, and trust Him Christ God, the Holy Spirit to fill you, to shield you and make the fear disappear. Let His Spirit fill you and resolve everything. He knows your needs; let it all go and trust in Him to provide.

Chapter 107

A lot more fun

You make the world you perceive. By not caring about your world, by not worrying, you are still going to do the things you do. However, if you act with courage and transmute your fears, it is a lot more fun and Christ will give you more happiness as you approach each aspect of your life.

So let go of the world of illusions. Do not play the miserable, empty, illusionary actor that fear and worry would have you be. Instead, do not care or worry and let fear go.

Remember, you can offer Christ God nothing; your hands are empty because you have been living in emptiness, in the illusion, in nothing. So let go of the illusionary past, let go of nothing, and let Christ's loving, living presence gift your eternal happiness and joy as you remember Him and return into Oneness with our Father.

Chapter 108

Wake up to Gods Will

Imagine waking up every day to God's Will. Each day, a perfect day.

Love's outcome is a battle of wills our will versus God's Will. We fail to choose God's Will only because we think we would have another: the will of the *imposter*, the *stranger*, the *thief in the night*.

Our will hides behind fear, behind our illusionary actions and deeds or so it seems. How can we do anything about "our will" when it does not exist, when it is tied up in an illusion?

Our will is an illusion, like everything else we perceive. Yet it seems to have consequences: our suffering and pain, the patterns we are stuck in day after day.

These consequences can be forgiven and not judged. They can be given away, as if confirming they never existed in the first place, and put back where they belong into Pandora's box, on the shelf, back into the illusion.

Here, it seems as though we are addressing the symptoms and not the cause of what is a disease. So we need to understand the cause so that we can be permanently healed and just be our true self.

If we could only be our true self always in Christ God's peace and love.

Our peace is like the surface of a lake. The wind blows and the waves form or so it seems. The harder the wind, the greater the waves, the greater the anxiety and pain.

We do not cause the waves. We do not cause the wind. They are illusions, but they seem to affect our peace. So it is with our will. We are not the cause of our will, yet we witness its effects.

So the question is: how do you stop the wind, the waves, and our illusionary will, when none of them exist?

We need to realise and believe that we are the creators of everything even dreams and illusions. The wind, the waves, our will, and our emotional state are all our creation.

Chapter 109

Your power is now seize it

There is power in the now. Outside the now, in the past and future, there are only illusions.

In the present is where Christ God works. The past and the future have no power and are illusory. They serve only, or so it seems, to imprison us all in the illusion, dreaming of the embryonic earth.

Our salvation is in the present, in the now. Not the past or the future, which are perceptions made from imaginary thoughts, powerless and the home of illusions.

Heaven's bus only stops in the now. So rest in being in the present and catch your ride home. Living in the present means you have to deal with unforgiveness trapped in your pain body. These will require commitment by yourself, in calmness, to meditate until they rise to the surface. Then you can shine the light of your forgiving presence on them to dissolve them away.

Having made it to living in the present now, the only thing that can knock you back into the dream is anxiety and worries, allowed to creep back in through your unguarded beingness. Anxiety leads to worry, then to the pain body and embryonic thoughts, with your awareness miles away from its pick-up point.

Non-judgement and forgiveness transmute fear into acceptance and love's presence. When love is present, so is timelessness.

"I never want this moment to end."

We only say this when we are in love's presence. "I don't want to lose this feeling. I don't care about anything and am happy to die into this moment rather than be removed from it."

And so, through continual forgiveness, we find our salvation and love, our true home. We must love to live and live in the present now, resting in our true safety.

Easier said than done, we have always held the key.

I guess the reason for my recurring dreams of missing my flight is all to do with this fact. My home is in the now. Whilst I continue to live worrying about the past and the future, I miss my flight home. I miss my only real life in the now.

So continually forgive away all your anxieties, doubts and concerns, and allow your life to blossom in the present now of Christ God's presence.

Chapter 110

Untarnished by sin

Every one of us remains perfect and untarnished by any sin or earthly perceptions and thoughts we seemingly have lived through. In other words, everything perceived and thought has had no effect on our innocent core, which remains in God as one combined, unified, unchangeable Will.

To look upon and feel our innocence internally and know God's Will, which is our own, we need only forgive away every earthly thought and everything perceived externally. We must remove the imposter whom we think we are, with its earthly thoughts.

So, without judgement, refocus with your forgiveness. Forgive away any anxieties and worrisome thoughts and stay living in the present, in the presence of God's Unified Will and Love. In this way, you experience yourself in Christ God and create your perfect day.

Chapter 111
All God's Children

We are all God's children, and because of unchecked fear and its associated earthly thoughts, we have forgotten who we are in truth. We have allowed ourselves, through the thoughts we accept, to imagine we are this earthly image we have made me, you, and all the inhabitants of the illusory embryonic earth.

Remember to reach into yourself every new day and transmute any fear that comes your way with your courage. Dispelling your imaginary earthly thoughts and perceptions, replace them with the love of Christ God's presence and the gifts He would will for us instead.

So forgive away any pain and judgements you hold onto, and embrace your true self in Christ.

Chapter 112

Cherish the Holy Son

Remember, all your judgements, all your thoughts, and all your unforgiveness create all you perceive around you, including your pain body which you can feel. All of this is fed by an undercurrent of fear projected at your awareness.

We need not worry about the false idols we worship in the world we perceive and create. Instead, we need only turn our gaze and cherish the Self that lies still, undamaged, at the core of our being: the Holy Son of God. The Holy Son, One in His Father, a real thing, the holy altar and the centre of our being. Worship that only, and know God's love for you, His Son. Upon receiving His Love, it is reflected in a new perception: a world beyond forgiveness, a sinless world perceived through newfound Christ Vision.

So remember, do not judge anything. Forgive away the outside illusory world you created, all of it, and allow yourself to turn your awareness inwards upon the Self – your true Self at the centre of your being. Experience yourself truly as God's child, your Father's love cherishing your sinlessness. At the same time, experience your love for Him with your new loving Christ Vision, fed by your eternal undercurrent of love.

Chapter 113

We remain connected to the Vine

The eternal flame that burns at the altar at the centre of our beingness is the same flame that burns in each and every one of us.

Like a pipeline with multiple outlets, we are all connected to our one source, and the brighter and more powerful our flame, so it is for everyone else as the flow of love is increased and felt by all.

The more anxiety and fear we transmute into love, the brighter our flame and the greater the love felt by each and every one. What we look upon shines brighter because of our gifts, just as our brothers' gifts increase us.

So, continue to create gifts for each other. Put on a smile, dress smartly, offer help when needed, give up your seat, and be gracious always.

The more we love each other, the more love is given to us from God, our source. The more gifts we give, the more gifts we receive from God as we give to others. And remember, when we give to others, we cannot lose, as we give to ourselves.

The salvation of humanity requires only that we all love and give to each other. God's salvation for us will be Christ's love for us: Christ's love, our love, God's love. We must want love to receive God's love through Christ our Saviour.

So, the message remains: keep working hard with your acts of forgiveness, kindness, courage and love. Salvation for you and all our brothers requires your love and presence in the now. Keep being a dutiful guard, converting fear into love with courage before it enters your beingness. And as a dutiful guard, be present to transmute any lingering fear hiding in your beingness, changing it into love with the light of your presence. Continually, in every instant, remain in the present and dissolve any anxieties in the presence of loving forgiveness.

So remain connected to the vine. Meditate into a state of calm beingness and go about your life without worrying about what you perceive. Stay in the present, be God's hardworking child, and transmute all your fears with love. And remember always to be guided by your compass of forgiveness and non-judgement towards your salvation in Christ God's love.

Chapter 114

Open your heart and feel

His peace and love surrounding you

Stop judging and worrying about what is not right in your multiverse. Instead, find the peace and love surrounding you in the present through your unconditional forgiveness, revealing all the gifts you and your brothers are in Christ God.

Remember, the instant you accept an earthly thought, your peace is disturbed. Be at peace and do not worry or think about what occurs outside of you. You are awareness itself. You are not your creation or the patterns that appear in your multiverse from the thoughts you accept.

So just be awareness itself and remember your true self, the witness in the sanctuary of your love, at peace and undisturbed by the emotions stirred by anxieties and thought patterns accepted by your mind and perceived externally in the Maya.

Remember, it is your forgiving presence that dissolves the emotional attachments, thoughts and patterns, making room for God's thoughts, peace and new experiences.

Chapter 115

Let Him fill you

Many people at some stage in their lives believe Christ God lives within them. Many are regularly filled with Christ's Holy Spirit and experience and know His truth throughout their lives.

Our single purpose is to return with that bit of Christ we feel inside us to its home. Christ's separated mind, each and every part of it, must return to God His Creator.

It is for God's Son to be a slave to time, to know of the embryonic earth, of good and evil, and of the mortal embryonic human experience. To know everything human. To know and understand every sin and every forgiveness.

Christ God, Christ in His Father and Creator, is the one only true consciousness: the Holy Spirit, the inner parent in each and every one of us.

So, given Christ's inseparable presence within His Father and in us, and never having wandered from the sure protection of His loving arms, the obvious question is: is it possible for those of us, from the mortal perspective, you and me, to experience God's protection all the time on earth, to rest in the Whole continually?

All the time meaning continually, instead of living in illusory exile. Living continually in the Holy Spirit, whilst seemingly also living here on earth, as long as the body breathes.

Jesus thought, taught and lived this way, and so have many of His followers. His message was very simple: do not worry about anything experienced in earthly time, forgive every sin and pain, and let the Holy Spirit fill you.

Christ's Holy Spirit has always been part of us and simply stands waiting in all of us, to be experienced fully in every moment, in place of slavery and wanting, in earthly time.

Chapter 116
Our Atonement

The Holy Spirit, who resides in the core of each and every one of us, on behalf of us all requests from His Creator atonement: the moment to save mankind and make itself whole in its Father through us, through all its parts, through the whole world, by salvation's means.

In other words, Christ knows He is incomplete until each and every one of us is restored to Him and His Father at the appointed hour.

Chapter 117
Humble Yourself

All my thoughts are arrogance. Even my best thoughts only point towards the truth whilst remaining a long distance off. Therefore, for salvation I must do away with my thoughts and fill the space created in my mind with God's thoughts only.

In other words, to let Christ God lead me and others home, I must let go of all my egoistic limiting thoughts, anxieties, fears and beliefs. Everything, no matter how much I value it, no matter how important, just or righteous I think it is, I must replace with the truth that only the Holy Spirit can give.

Invite the Holy Spirit to fill your beingness, replacing the space vacated by your ego-driven false self.

Chapter 118

Your never alone

How fortunate we all are that we are never alone. God's Holy Son lives inside all of us. He Himself is of one Will, in unity with His Father.

All we need to do is experience Him continually throughout the day. Have a relationship with Him.

Remember, He is always present, like a magical genie. So let love replace fear. Let the Holy Spirit, our inner heavenly parent, provide everything Heaven can give.

Remove all obstacles blocking the Holy Spirit from making real positive changes in your life. Remove the ego's limiting expectations by expecting nothing from its world.

With your courage, forgive away all anxieties and fears, and do not worry or care about the ego's fearful world. Witness with your newfound faith as your life is transformed by the Holy Spirit, God's Son, your true self.

Chapter 119

Fear power or Gods Love power, you choose

There is no will except the Will of Love. God's Will of Love.

Fear power is how much effort our host seems prepared to make in the dream to run away from danger, fearful perceptions and death. We mistakenly think we have a separate will.

Only God has a Will, the Will to create through Love. Love power. We have the complete opposite. No will, just our robotic reactions to fearful ideas flowing into our awareness. These ideas stem from anxieties felt by our host, our illusionary body, the cause of all the manifestations, perceptions and thoughts created in our illusionary brains, the only place where our host can create an image of the external, what it thinks is outside of it. At best, our brains can be likened to a periscope connected to our gut with a foghorn accessory sounding the alarm every time the ego feels threatened.

This is probably why we never seem to progress on our spiritual journey home to our Creator, no matter how much we try. We are running in the wrong direction. We mistakenly think we have a separate willpower that will take our journey to Him when we have none. All we have is fear power, creating more dreams and causing us to run towards what we are trying to escape from, running back towards the fire.

Watch yourself and others running around repeating the same behaviour, like zombies possessed by fear, acting out the same patterns each and every day. We are all possessed.

This reminds me of a quotation from Jesus where He talked about removing the stick from your own eye before you point out the faults of others.

Chapter 120

The puppet

As clear as the stars at night, when the clouds of fear have drifted out of our minds, God's truth is everywhere. Every gift He created waits for us, hidden by our illusions and lies, a thick veil masking our truth, just waiting for the light of our presence to reveal everything true which He has gifted.

Remember, we need only transmute fear and illusions to see in the light of our true presence with Christ Vision.

So forgive away fear, and with your acceptance, non-judgement, courage and knowledge that everything is illusion, designed to bait, find freedom in Christ God, your true Self. You just need to peel away the layers upon layers of illusions and temptations, designed to mask the pain of separation from our Creator. Designed by a devil of sorts to tempt and imprison us in the embryonic savage earth to know of good and evil.

So, confidently and happily each day, remind yourself to be present and without judgement. Bid the devil and its illusions goodbye, with your acceptance, with your forgiveness of anxieties and fears, with non-judgement and love.

Forgive all the pains of separation away as you forgive away all your idols.

In the children's story of *Pinocchio*, Pinocchio wanted to belong somewhere. Somewhere turned out to be his true self, a real boy, not a puppet. The toymaker, his creator, wanted a real boy, a son, and the puppet was the nearest thing he could create with His Own Will. To have a real son, Pinocchio needed to create his own will.

Naïve and unknowing, Pinocchio was quickly fooled by the wolf. He was lost, could not find his creator, and to hide the pain was quickly led into temptations at the island fairground. The island is symbolic of his separation from his creator, where temptations usurp the mind.

The growing nose symbolised each bait leading to another bait, one temptation after another. Everyone yearns for their true home, not illusions. Your home is where there is no more pain, not somewhere which conceals pain with temptations.

So, no more being the devil's puppet, taking bait after bait. Like Pinocchio, leave the island. Convert all the anxieties and pain by forgiving them away. Rid yourself of temptations and illusions and return to your Creator as your true self with your own will and your own purpose. Your Will to create with your Father's shared Will in shared Mind.

So gain your freedom, and end your separation by looking through the veil with non-judgemental, loving acceptance and forgiveness.

Remember, food, alcohol, drugs, sex, your human body, your family, your friends everything is a poor substitute, made imperfect by your addictions to mask the pain of separation, providing temporary relief in the illusion of temptations.

Chapter 121
The original fear

Fear: do not hide from it. Instead, forgive it away before it enters your being and awareness.

When you are not looking, when you are not on your guard, in unconsciousness and darkness, fear invades your beingness, causing you to cower like a mole and bury yourself in all your earthly temptations and idols of choice, everything you have created to hide from the fear and escape. Even frailty and death become a final hiding place once the illusory human strength you placed your faith in has finally run out.

So darkness must be met with light. The light of your presence alone will dissipate fear. Forgive it away and bring joy and remembrance of our Creator. God asks that we reach into our beingness with courage and shine the light of our presence on all darkness and all the illusions that our unchallenged fears have created after slipping covertly into our beingness to mask our happiness when anxieties were let into our being and into our awareness.

The only thing He asks is that we forgive away the original pain of separation, the original fear which remains hiding in our beingness to this day, having eaten from the so called forbidden fruit temptations we still pursue. Like a room whose curtains have been drawn closed for centuries, dissolve the pain with the light of your presence. Let it lift the veil and let God's Son's heavenly light, joy and love flow into your beingness for the salvation of the world.

At various stages of our illusory lives, pivotal events can occur. For example, loss of lifelong friendships or partners, loss of a job or retirement, war, and loss of all worldly goods and money. All these have the potential to leave a gaping void in our illusory lives, leading to acute emotional pain and depression.

There are times in our lives when the original pain of separation from our Creator is revealed, like waves washing away the sands that cover the ancient hidden cause of our separation from God our Father. When fully understood, the illusions and temptations can be seen for what they are, just temporary fixes. Known to drug addicts but unknown to most of us, we have filled our lives with temporary fixes to hide intense pain. Unknown to almost everyone, this is the original pain of separation.

We can run away from the pain, and most do, normally by creating more illusions: getting another job or another partner, seeking more money, or even suicide anything and everything to keep running away from the original pain. This is the opportunity for your resurrection, your return to God and love.

The original same pain is now partially exposed for you to see. Now, with all your strength, reach into yourself, find more courage, and turn your awareness away from cowering. Meet the pain head on, blasting it with your unconditional forgiveness, your heavenly light and full presence. Filled now with the Holy Spirit, turn your light on all your remaining illusions, light them all up and, with fasting and abstinence, light up the whole world with your Heavenly free flowing Love.

Chapter 122
The miracles making - be careful what you wish for

Thoughts are ideas accepted and rooted in our minds. For example, an image of a house, manifested from an initial idea, created into our illusionary multiverse and held onto as our own.

Once accepted by our minds, an idea becomes a thought that is fed into a miraculous process of sorts to manifest in our illusionary perception for our awareness to behold.

In truth, the idea started before, as an anxiety. *Where do I live? Where do I find shelter? What shall I eat and drink?* Anxiety always starts in the gut, a hunger, taking root and becoming the source of all our illusions and wants. It always turns into a poor version of what you might picture until you have completely forgiven away the gut feeling and associated doubting thoughts, leaving your mind clear for Christ God to create and for you to witness the miracle taking form.

Christ God is never far from you, closer than your own thoughts, working tirelessly to manifest everything you want.

When you think about it this way, our whole seeming experience, our life, is one miraculous, magical, continuous process of ideas accepted as thoughts, then perceived as real and our own through Christ God.

It is important to discipline our minds to accept the ideas we want. If our ideas and thoughts are to want God to lead us home, then we must make room in our minds for His idea by ridding ourselves of the mundane, looping, useless thoughts that create perceptions which serve no benefit and obscure our relationship to Him.

So, take ownership of your mind. In other words, be the guardian of your mind by filtering the ideas it accepts. The opposite is to be brainwashed, easily manipulated and controlled by hateful ideas streaming into our minds uncontrolled, leading to awful, frightening images. These are then projected outwardly, creating a miserable world little more than a prison.

If you are sick and tired of the perceptions, the unpleasant things you witness, the events in your life, then change the ideas. Forgive away the anxiety in your gut first to change the thoughts you accept, thus changing your perceptions and your patterns.

Patterns are the repeating of mistakes. Being stuck in a situation you are unhappy with happens because you keep accepting the same ideas in your mind. Remove the anxiety first and create space in your mind for God's shared thoughts.

Remember, in your creation, God has ready for you every gift of mankind He has. This means every idea associated with mankind, including poverty, wealth, family, enemies and friends. Everything apparent in your life stems from ideas.

To you, His child, He held nothing back. There are no secret closets of human or earthly knowledge hidden out of view, no hidden ideas, no hidden gifts of mankind.

God's gifts are ideas, and the ideas you accept create outwardly in the world you will perceive. He provided us with the ability to create anything from ideas.

Imagine a coffee machine that can produce an infinite number of coffee flavours from a store of infinite capsules. Your mind is the coffee machine, and the capsules are the ideas. Your willpower is the hand that selects the capsule based on knowledge and experience of the flavours.

It is hard to believe, but I suppose this is the essence of faith: knowing and believing you create from the ideas you value and keep close to your heart.

This reminds me of a Jesus quotation where he compared one's actions to the fruit one would bear. In other words, the ideas you store and value in your mind will show outwardly, producing good or bad outcomes in your life.

So, everything outwardly, everything you perceive, is not done to you. Everything outwardly, you create. You manifest the ideas you value. Everything here means everything.

Everything starts with an anxious gut feeling, which becomes an idea in your mind, then takes root and manifests in your awareness. The world we think we see is created by ideas, God's gifts.

This popular saying is so true: *be careful what you wish for.*

All ideas have the potential to become good or bad gifts as they manifest in our multiverse. We have been created with the ability to turn any idea into perceptions, images, sounds, and so on.

We most definitely also have the power to create and witness any idea by leaving the doors of our minds wide open.

So, without judging, continually guard your mind and choose carefully what you want to know. If you do not want to know devilish things, do not accept devilish ideas.

Just because you have an open mind does not mean you have to create every idea that enters. That is why the hippy movement got lost. Their open-mindedness let in ideas of drug and substance abuse.

So, be open-minded, but always be on guard. Be the master, not the puppet. Be in control of your mind.

Learn to take back control of your mind by practising resisting temptations. Resisting certain ideas. Abstain from a thought, and you cease to manifest the idea. This is why fasting is so good for you. Fasting leads to a stronger mind and a stronger will, as you rid yourself of the anxiety that would draw you to the temptation in the first instance. Fasting brings the strength and peace of mind required to control ideas and their manifestations.

So, take ownership of your mind and your outwardly transpiring multiverse.

There is nothing and no one to blame for your perceptions but yourself. However, do not judge or blame yourself.

You create your multiverse. You are the creator of everything you witness in your awareness by your acceptance of the ideas leading up to every perception. Remember, everything living and non-living in your awareness you create and sustain with further ideas you accept.

What you think to blame as some other devil's creation is your own creation. What you witness, see and hear are your ideas.

Take ownership, because they became your thoughts the instant you accepted them. All thoughts given are gifted, whether good or evil. Each of us is literally like Pandora. Uncontrolled ideas always lead to mayhem.

As you witness the perceptions in your life, learn to accept them without judging. This way, you take away the creative power of an idea you do not want. If you judge the idea, you make it your own and keep playing it over and over in your mind, for it to keep repeatedly manifesting in your multiverse.

Imagine you are in God's Library, and you want to find something interesting to learn. In this special library, all the learning books are read by fully immersing your mind in the ideas they contain.

For our current situation here on earth, it is time to remember this and how we became immersed in mankind in the first place.

It is time to exit the book in God's Library titled *Mankind and the Embryonic Earth – To Learn of Good and Evil Through Temptations*.

Our salvation, and the salvation of our world, requires that we stop feeding ourselves with devilish thoughts.

The book of mankind is nearing its end. It is time to bring our awareness out of this book.

We take our awareness out of the book by taking back control of our minds. So, there is no need to worry about any of the devilish thoughts or their seeming manifestations and illusions.

Detach from all these ideas, and trust and accept the new ideas that God will provide. He knows what we need and will provide those ideas for us to create.

It is on us to create instead what God Wills, by disciplining our minds to accept His ideas and His thoughts, and to create heaven, the opposite of hell, here on earth in our multiverse.

Let your love flow always, no matter what you seemingly witness, by not accepting hateful ideas.

Create and witness what you want your multiverse to be. Clean your slate.

Be yourself. Be love and peace instead of hate and anger.

Replace all your ideas of hate with new ideas, new gifts, continually, confidently, acceptingly, and without judging.

Take away the power from your devilish creations by denying their ideas with forgiveness, replacing hate and judgement with love and acceptance. Bring the wheels of your hell to a grinding halt and steer a different course for your awareness, where the salvation of your world becomes your true vision.

Chapter 123

He is my Brother

Our salvation will soon be upon us with the arrival of our Creator's Son, who is our brother. Like any elder brother who loves His Father and His family, He will lead us all home at the appointed hour.

Chapter 124

Be Patient

A child, impatient and desperately wanting to rush ahead, is guided by its emotions to experience life, but in its enthusiasm keeps tripping and suffering in the woes of the earth, repeatedly making the same mistakes, falling to the same temptations and repeating the same patterns.

Instead, the child could walk by the side of its parents from time to time, at least until it is more experienced and ready to take on life's challenges, carrying their wisdom and guidance forward for both itself and for its future children.

Before we do anything, even before going to sleep or studying, focus on Heaven, the second place where God's Will and our will are One. In other words, give thanks to our cosmic embryonic ancestors and the earth the first place accept and leave all judgements behind, and in forgiveness of all things in the first place, rest in the unified Divine Will, Love, Peace and Guidance the second place.

Chapter 125

Losing our focus

Remember, temptations are like adhesives that glue us to the imperfect earth through ideas we accept, such as judgements, hatred, non-acceptance and unforgiveness.

Earthly perception is therefore a consequence of our vision having lost its focus after accepting and harbouring earthly ideas. The opposite is Christ Vision and salvation, remaining focused on God's thoughts while continually forgiving, not judging, accepting, showing gratitude and loving everything that comes into your awareness as you give thanks and lovingly release yourself from fear.

It is like placing your trust in a fleshy primitive brain tripping on errors instead of trusting God's thoughts where only Divine Truth abides. Imagine your mind with impaired vision fearfully driving on a moonless night with torrential rain covering your windscreen when instead you could journey on a calm sunny day, every day, with 20/20 Christ Vision through the lens of God's thoughts.

So confidently and happily, with thanks, forgive away every anxiety in your multiverse. Do not worry about a thing or any of the ghostly shadows you have experienced in the fearful dream of perception. Instead, trust in God our Creator and Father and know your multiverse in your loving forgiving light. Look through the veil with 20/20 vision, with nothing but closure and gratitude for our ghostly cosmic ancestors, as your loving forgiveness transforms into Christ Vision for the salvation of the Son of God, your true self abiding in you and in each and every one of your brothers as you release them too from the prison you made.

Chapter 126
Ghostly thoughts

Devils' thoughts, or whatever you want to call them I prefer to call them the ghostly thoughts of our cosmic ancestors are the thoughts our minds accept and use to create the world we witness and the world they evolved in.

So it seems we are subjected to an endless stream of seemingly real thoughts which create in our minds the sinful, illusionary world we imagine and think we see each and every day. With apparently no end to these thoughts, it is only when we willfully forgive them away that we are then able to be one Will with our Creator and restore His shared, real thoughts, which Christ God, our true self, would reveal. With this Vision Christ Vision our sight changes from earthly perception to Heavenly Vision where sin, imperfection and wanting are no longer perceived and we have willed that our joyful Heavenly thoughts alone are accepted in our minds in our Oneness in our Father.

So each day, each moment, do not worry about anything you perceive and simply forgive everything away. Do not care about anything as our vision is restored by God's Heavenly thoughts.

Chapter 127

The pickpocket

The Holy Spirit sees only sinlessness. We, like Him, must do likewise despite being impelled by outside forces to do otherwise.

Outside forces are earthly, anxiety-driven ideas that are allowed to form and take root in our gut before taking form in our unguarded mind the causation of all our perceptions and unhappiness.

With effort, courage and your loving presence, the light of your forgiveness dispels earthly anxiety-driven thoughts, changing your perceptions, your patterns and your earthly creations that which you look upon day in, day out.

Forgiveness, acceptance and trust bring your presence, your light and your lit-up mind to the fore, illuminating your mind and everything you look upon in your multiverse.

Remember, Heaven is priceless. It can never be bought or possessed. But forgiveness, acceptance and trust in God, when you expect the least, provides and gets you a ticket to ride in joy.

Heaven is made up of an infinite number of forgiven ideas, zillions upon zillions. Its opposite, hell the embryonic earth is made up of an equal number of unforgiven ideas. Christ taught we get to have Heaven now. A ticket to ride now. There is no need to wait.

Total forgiveness, acceptance and trust in God to provide draws your aliveness to the front, no longer hidden beneath layers and layers of fear and doubt. Forgiveness, acceptance and trust removes the stick in your eye, ensuring your vision is in holy light and not in the darkness of a fearful mind.

In the holy light of your presence you then remember to see your brothers and yourself in sinlessness with Christ Vision, just as you were created by our Creator, whose Oneness in truth we also remember we are part of and whose thoughts we gladly accept for our everlasting joy and freedom.

So, in summary, remain continually in a state of forgiveness. Forgive away your anxieties and fears before they take root. Be the guardian of your mind, forgiving away any earthly ideas which would otherwise settle and create perceptions of unhappiness, non-acceptance and mistrust. Remain in a permanent state of undoubting mind, accepting our Creator's ideas for our external peace and joy.

It is like every idea has a price to pay for its Heavenly transmutation to eternal joy. That price is forgiveness, acceptance and trust to move on to its opposite Heavenly transmutation.

Temptation is like the pickpocket that robs you of your joy, leading to a sense of loss and sadness. But temptation is worse than that, for as it takes over your mind its ideas take root and rob you further, a parasite dragging you down into a rabbit hole of darkness and more unchecked, unforgiven earthy thoughts, leading to the loss of all remembrance of our Father and causing us to see our brother and ourselves in the poorest version of each other.

Like a worm virus infecting a computer, our mind becomes corrupted, blind and lost to anxiety and fear.

So stay in forgiveness, acceptance and trust and experience your multiverse in Christ Vision as you see and remember your brothers and yourself in sinlessness, as one with our Creator, our eternal Heavenly Home.

Chapter 128

Be the happiest child in the room

We need to switch from perception, which is to see our world, our multiverse, as poor, wanting and imperfect, and get on board with and enjoy our lives confidently and happily in Christ God with Christ Vision and Our Truth.

The switch from perception to Christ God Vision is a definite break. It is a decision, a decision to want to be happy, to live in Christ-hood, to be the happiest child in the room. It is one or the other. You make the commitment to go there and, through living, you may falter with worry or doubt and not get there. Or you contain your worry with courage, forgive away all anxieties and fears before they take root, and you get there.

So, in Oneness with our Father, we must allow our Father's Heavenly Thoughts to replace those thoughts of our suffering embryonic earthly ancestors that we allowed into our minds. At the same time, we must remain in thanks always for their sacrifice. Then we must forgive away all their worrying thoughts and pain and, joyfully and continually, whilst trusting in God to provide all the rewards, acknowledge that their sacrifice gave us, their future generations, us the immortals.

So, remember to stop mourning the world you think you live in. It is dead and gone. Your host is dead and gone. Our ancestors and everything you think you are died zillions upon zillions of years ago.

Live happily with thanks so their sacrifice was not all for nothing. Start living in the present, the now, residing in our Creator.

You could say there are two ways of living: the dark side, hell, in the past the world of our embryonic earthly existence or the bright side, Heaven, the present.

Take ownership of everything, own your life. With your forgiveness, let the past go and keep facing the present moment.

So, no longer turn your back on our Creator. Embrace Him and create your own Heaven now, trusting He will provide everything you need by thankfully, confidently and happily accepting every gift He has created for you in your unlimited treasure store.

Chapter 129

Atone and let your sinlessness be know

Atonement is the restoration of our trust in Him, God's Son, and our understanding that He lives in us in sinlessness, despite the false image we create of our Self.

Accept everything, good or bad, to keep clarity of mind and remembrance of forgiveness to forgive away everything without judging. When you do not accept or forgive and instead judge, you accumulate further worry and pain. So, treat everything as a lesson, accept it and move on with your forgiveness unwavering.

When you have forgiven away every anxiety, every fear, every illusionary image of yourself, every false idol, all the earthly thoughts that plagued and usurped your mind and denied your memory of your Self and our Father, only then will your Atonement be complete and your sinlessness be known.

We need only trust our Father and understand He gifts us everything we expect. Everything is our creation, as we expect. Happiness or unhappiness all our own expectations met. If we do not want more of anything, we need only forgive it away. We do not need to worry; we detach from it. God's gifts are precisely everything we expect.

So, in summary, let love and trust guide us inwards to happiness, away from fear and doubt, back to our Source.

And remember, non-acceptance, judging, fear and doubt draw us deeper into earthly temptation, unhappiness, the external, the illusion, the dream of separation, away from love and trust, from remembrance of our Source, and towards everything we expect in the embryonic earth.

Your aim is to expect nothing. If you expect, you create the dream. Instead, do not expect and know your sinlessness. Know your Self.

Chapter 130

Pull out the weeds

There is only one way to receive God's Thought of salvation, and that is to have no other thought in your mind.

Remember, thoughts create as ideas are allowed by your self to settle on your mind. It is like your mind is fertile soil.

You manifest the ideas you plant. But they are not really ideas you deliberately plant. They are ideas blowing in the wind, figuratively speaking, because of your lack of presence, allowed to settle on your mind and then appearing in your perception. Seeds from weeds that land on your mind weed-ideas, perceptions of the embryonic earth.

So, guard your field, guard your mind, by simply being continually present.

Do not judge. Judgement is like grasping at the seeds of weeds flying around in the wind and then sowing them yourself, reinforcing earthly ideas in your mind. Do not let the seeds of weeds take root in your mind. Do not expect and grow the imperfect, bad manifestations of misery and unhappiness in your perception.

Trust God to provide. Keep your field your mind clear of earthly thoughts and let His idea take root in your mind. Follow His Thought, its scent is Love. Follow love by not worrying or judging, and if any weeds are spotted, slipping in through temptations and distractions, wake up, refocus and forgive them away along with all their manifestations.

As you become more present, you become sharper at spotting the earthly thoughts that have grown and hidden themselves in your flower beds. Learn to pick them out. Forgive anxieties and fears away before they produce seeds, more weeds, more pain and more misery.

In place of your judgements, witness miracles of happiness from seeds of joy which only God's Thoughts provide. So, happily and joyfully, forgive away every earthly thought you did not mean to plant.

Judging this world is like stepping from one weed patch into another weed patch, from imperfection to imperfection, growing weeds instead of flowers.

It is time to wake up from earthly thoughts to God's perfect Thoughts, and it takes effort. Just be present and guard your mind, and bask in the Son Light and Oneness of the Son of God, your true sinless Self.

Chapter 131

Transmute your anxieties with courage into love

You can only be fearless, that is, completely free from fear, not by hiding from fear or burying it within, but by being present and transmuting every anxiety and fear into love. Eventually, you will transmute all fear into love, like the progress bar on a computer screen as you download a file.

Then, when complete fearlessness is achieved, your salvation is certain, all fear transmuted by your courage into love.

Your lack of presence allows anxiety and fearful ideas to cause pain to be added to your pain body and to form devilish thoughts in your mind. These create bad perceptions, more pain and unhappiness, things you do not really want, but because you accepted the anxiety and thought, you created them in your perception.

It is like leaving the front door wide open to the street whilst you are not at home. Whilst you are gone, that is, not present, bad thoughts invade your home, invade your mind and settle, making themselves comfortable and inviting more stranger thoughts into your home, into your mind, into your sanctuary.

Only after you have evicted all the bad thoughts, thoughts of the embryonic earth, are you left with a clean house, a pure mind, uncorrupted and operating in the One Thought you share with Christ God.

Remember, fear's transmutation with forgiveness into love draws your presence to the fore, revealing your true self in *Christhood* and our Oneness in our Father.

So, when you are confused, angry, upset or out of integrity, remember to refocus, calm your beingness, and accept that your perceptions are your creation, created from the strange thoughts you let into your mind whilst you were *comfortable, tempted, unguarded.*

Chapter 132

One Soul is all it takes

Anxiety, fear, earthly thoughts and perceptions create ripples, waves and storms in all our minds, leading to the loss of stillness, oneness and sinlessness. The lake, the sum of all our seemingly separated parts, is lost in a fearful storm, losing sight of our Father's glowing, loving light.

Yet just one part, one soul, one separated mind can have the courage and strength to forgive away all thoughts of sin in all of its brothers, all of its parts, to see and unify once again love's reflection, restoring peace to all the parts, all the souls, all of his brothers in all of his Father's creation. He restores unto Himself His Holiness, reflecting back on Him from all His creation, unified in understanding and saved at last in the salvation of the Son of God.

Chapter 133

Love is all we can carry

It is love that created Heaven and all of creation, and as such our salvation—our stepping through the door, so to speak, to our home—can only be with love filling our entire beingness. So it remains that we must leave everything that is not love behind. All anxieties, fear, anger and judgement belong to the embryonic earth and embryonic mankind, our cosmic ancestors. Only love is carried through the Heavenly gate.

Like some sort of cosmic alien space ship, God harvests only love from all of His creations. Yet once we step into the light of His truth, we will understand in love's oneness that we saved ourselves. Our total forgiveness will remind us who we have always been.

So forgive away every emotion that is not love. Keep your awareness watchful of your mind and prevent judgement, earthly thoughts and doubts that would keep pulling you back from taking the final step into God's ocean of love. In that instant when you take the final step, you will take your brothers with you, for their minds, through your understanding, are lit up with the blazing truth of God's plan for everyone's salvation. Not one is left behind as the mind of the Son is restored, unified with all its separated parts, all of its brothers, and one with the Father.

Chapter 134

Your Holy Sanctuary awaits you undefiled

Your Holy Sanctuary remains undefiled. This means you can reclaim, at any time, its unlimited peace and love. Only you, God's child, are the master of everything you experience. With your love freely flowing, God's holy gifts—your peace and happiness—are assured as your creative power transitions to limitless in your co-existence with our Creator.

Love's opposite is fear, and all its derivatives—non-acceptance, anger, hate and all their associated thoughts—can quickly blindside you, transforming your multiverse into darkness as you forget who you are. Your tranquil beingness is turned inside out, from peace into turmoil, from oneness with our Father to isolation, and from abundance to seeming limitation, as all your expectations now seemingly align with alien thoughts adopted by your mind. Your heaven is transformed into the embryonic earth exactly as your mind, now immersed in earthly thoughts, expects. All around you, life becomes a burden, becomes your enemy, becomes your prison with meagre offerings, and death appears as an illusory means of escape.

So transform your multiverse and save yourself in God's oneness. Let your multiverse, in love's presence once again, produce the fruit of your happy one mind in Christ God—no longer sour or distasteful, and no longer fearful of displacing your own presence.

Do not let fear push you around and out of your house. When fear comes knocking, do not hide your presence and let it take over your multiverse, turning it once again into unhappiness and making you its product, dragging you by your feet into its darkness.

Instead, stand tall, be confident, forgive everything and surf with love. Your presence is all that is needed—never alone and always filled with the Holiness of Your Oneness, the Holy Spirit—everything that is needed to light up fear's darkness and keep your multiverse in Heaven.

So, in summary, make it your goal to remember this day and every day until time drifts into timelessness: everything created in your multiverse is exactly as your mind expects. In the light of continual total forgiveness, keep your loving light present always in the foreground. Keep yourself present in the foreground where you, in your Father, create with His shared thoughts everything your beautiful One Mind has in store for you.

Chapter 135

Tap the Source of Love Itself

As we perceive, we are using earthly ideas directed towards our mind, creating the embryonic earth in our perception, or from sinlessness, our Creator's love and thoughts at the centre of our beingness.

So remember, always in the dream, you are the only witness. The only observer of your mind's thoughts. You alone are aware of the dream you dream, the dream you create. However much you think your dream is real, each of the actors, including your host and the hosts of all your loved ones, enemies, everything and everyone, are illusionary, or, to use a kinder description, earthly ghosts of characters long dead for over zillions upon zillions of years. I am reminded here of Jesus's words, *"Let the dead bury the dead."*

In the dream, your unguarded mind is creating from thoughts of the embryonic earth and characters that existed and died a very, very long time ago, and creating all of your perceptions.

Heaven's treasures are seen only in Christ Vision, with love as the power source, so to speak. The truth is created by love, direct from the source of truth in our Oneness with our Creator, when you have guarded your mind and created space for God's thoughts and love to land, undiluted by earthly thoughts on our minds — *the wheat separated from the chaff.*

Therefore, to experience true vision and not illusion, it is for your mind to continually tap the source of love itself, the sanctuary from which love flows from our Creator and whose source is sinlessness. This is the love that has flowed forever to all those saved before us and to all those who will be saved after our salvation and have awakened from the dream of the earth.

I suppose if you are the only witness of your life, your multiverse and dream, then giving to your brother is giving to yourself, just as forgiving your brother is forgiving yourself. By extension, not forgiving your brother is not forgiving yourself, as being angry or hateful towards your brother is being angry and hateful towards yourself.

Thus it follows that to continually forgive and love all things in your multiverse, in your life, is to continually forgive and love yourself from the source of love and creation, which is your Oneness with our Creator.

It is a bit like trying to get a job after spending years at school or college and, with no work experience, finding that prospective employers doubt the applicant's usefulness. But how can they get experience without being given an opportunity to gain experience? Yet most do get jobs, as they glow in the light of love's creation which their prospective employer sees and seeks, even if they do not know it. The light of love is the same light that comes from sinlessness. Applicants have no experience and therefore no doubts in that situation. They have no baggage, so to speak, their light and love flowing visibly.

Whilst they are easily moulded at work (in their earthly dream), they can keep their authenticity by staying true to love only. With time passing, they can excel at the job, with love as their guide, and be gifted more and more earthly rewards. Doubts will always start to plague them, like the rest of us, but eventually, they will see that only love creates, and that life only comes from inside them, not from anything they perceive in the dream — that is, anything external to them created by their earthly anxieties, fears and thoughts.

For God's Son's graduation into Heaven, His CV must have A-stars in every single earthly experience. In other words, He must be fully experienced and focused in transmuting every anxiety and fearful idea before they can take root in His mind, to dwell permanently in the sanctuary of love with His Father and put an end to His and our earthly dreams.

As you try to live in truth each day, in joy, remember the transition from dream to Christ Vision happens only when you have detached fully, one hundred per cent, from the earthly situation in which you currently find yourself. That means no earthly ideas are allowed by you to settle on your guarded mind, making room for your love only to create in your mind.

So continually forgive away the earthly anxieties and ideas that, like weeds, will try again and again to plant and re-plant themselves in your mind, creating unhappiness. Continually disregard them and let your continuous, unconditional love instead be your only true source of creation, as it overflows into your multiverse from the sanctuary and source of love, providing salvation for your mind and all your brothers in the shared Oneness we all have with our Creator.

So remember, absolutely everything in your multiverse is your creation. At every moment since your creation, your mind has had the choice to create from two separate sources: the easy source, the wide door, which is anxiety, fear, earthly ideas and doubt — as Jesus called them, *"the thoughts of the devil"* — or the ideas of the embryonic earth, as I call it, whose fruits are temptations, unhappiness, isolation, sin, sickness, evil and death. Or you may create from love, whose source is the sanctuary of love, from God's shared thoughts, freely given to us in Oneness to create, and whose fruits are truth, happiness, joy, Christ Vision and salvation.

Jesus taught those who would listen to continually create happiness with their unconditional love flowing through their minds, created by their unconditional forgiveness. Unconditional means without doubts mixed in. They would therefore prepare, purify their minds with their unconditional forgiveness, creating room for God's shared thoughts to land.

So simply make it your purpose, your continual intention, to create from love instead of doubt by continually, with courage, guarding your mind and forgiving away every fearful thought before it lands on your mind to create evil in your perception.

It is like a passenger train, the engine carriage being the mind powered by anxieties, fear and doubts, pulling carriages full of more anxieties, fears and doubts, and always closed-minded on tracks running around in constant circles, never getting anywhere, forced only to stop when faced with disaster or when experiencing disaster. Recognise the signals God puts up in front of your journey, the signposts to switch to love's power, avoiding further anxieties, fearful thoughts and pain as you head straight home with salvation for you and all your fellow passengers. This reminds me of the miraculous plane landings we hear about, made by courageous pilots when faced with disaster and certain death, or the one or handful of passengers and crew who walked out of impossible situations.

Live with love's power and be cloaked in the protection of the Holy Spirit.

Chapter 136

Restored to Unity

More than ever I am convinced that everything perceived is dreamt and created from thoughts allowed to settle on my mind.

Absolutely everything, the whole world, including my body, all my loved ones, what I think I am, everything, is a subset of thoughts in the mind of the Son of God. Everyone else I perceive is exactly the same, living in a different but similar subset of thoughts in the mind of God's Child.

It is for the Son of God to awaken from His dream so that all of us, His fragmented mind, can be restored to peace. At some point in time, when the Son of God's learning is complete, His Father will switch off the earth we knew and a new earth will be born as His Son awakens in Him. And each and every one of us, every subset of His Mind, will be restored to unity in Him, each other and the Father as One Being.

So do not worry about anything imagined. Forgive it all away, everything earthly, all temptations. Do not hold on to pain or old wounds. Instead, detach from the anxiety and thoughts creating them, and make room in your mind to feel the radiance of God's Love reflecting on You and the whole world as the world counts down towards our reunification in God's One Love.

Chapter 137
The fake will

We seemingly have two wills: one we share with the Son and the Father, and the other, the ego, the thief in the night, who covertly substitutes the Son of God's shared creative Will with His Father with its fake will, its ideas and perceptions, keeping us imprisoned in the dream of the embryonic earth.

We never progress in our spiritual journey home because we keep forgetting to forgive away the earthly thoughts that constantly usurp our awareness with the dream of earth. Only when we fully accept and follow the Son of God as our direction and truth, with His shared Thoughts with God, are we able to escape the ego's thoughts and the dream of the embryonic earth.

Be ruthless. Leave everything behind, all illusions, your earthly perception of everyone, and reach freedom, peace and salvation for everyone and yourself in the protection of the Holy Spirit. The earth is your ego's self-imposed prison, whilst Heaven is your true Home. Your awareness cannot be in both at the same time. You cannot mix the imperfect and lacking with perfection that has everything.

When your back is to the wall and you are hungry to survive, your natural instinct is not to think, not to worry, not to panic, but to detach from anxiety, to live in the present moment and do something constructive to meet the need. You discard all feelings about the situation you are confronted with and are simply the silent observer, doing what needs to be done. You have created in silence a space for the prey to wander into. You are the predator, ready to pounce on your prey.

Praying is wanting to know truth. It is forgiving away anxieties, fears and fearful thoughts. It is simulating that hunger moment. It is living in the present moment, setting aside earthly anxieties, thoughts and doubts. It is listening. It is creating space in your mind for God's shared Thoughts to fill. It is following Christ God, your true self. It is allowing God's shared Will to lead you.

So let your ego's will be hungry for a miracle only, and let your mind be still, just as if it is on a hunt and a sacrifice is needed, the mind guarding itself, making room for God's Thoughts to pounce. Everything external is forgiven away so the prayer can be had in Christ God, the miracle received as you act in the Holy Spirit. The lion lying down with the lamb in green pastures.

Chapter 138

Gift your body to Christ

Our Heavenly Home, a state of ecstatic existence, is the complete opposite of life on earth, full of expectations. For the body and ego, everything external on earth is meant to be exactly as instinctively expected, to keep the body feeling safe, as it would have been on the embryonic earth. If suddenly something truly unexpected happened, it would cause overwhelming fear, panic, or a shocking of the brain into silence — a last resort to blank out the experience completely, keeping the brain safe with no future memory of the event, and no memory preventing the reliving of it every day.

With practice, the body and brain can be trained to expect nothing, with the body continually in a state of calm, free from fear, aware but with no expectations, and at the same time capable of being a conduit for its Higher Self, whose *gifts* and *miracles* replace the space previously filled with expectations in its mind.

If preconceived ideas in the play of life, are the expectations made in the external by the mind at the earthly level, then miracles are ideas gifted by the Higher Self to itself, Christ God to Christ

God, God's Will for its pleasure and made visible in the external by the suspension of the preconceived ideas of the host. *Like a blip in the world of expectation.*

So the host never witnesses the miracle. It only knows of its occurrence from the witness testimonies of those experiencing the event through seeing, hearing, feeling, or any combination of these senses. This explains why the host is always unconscious of the event. The host will always be seemingly unaware of its normal external environment, sometimes still, sometimes trance-like, or ecstatic. Mostly, in ecstatic trance, their bodies seem stuck in awe of the appearance in their vision, their awareness. It can also happen when seemingly asleep, the sleeping American prophet. The host is always unaware. The brain is unaware, seemingly deploying the same safety mechanism as it would if an extremely fearful event occurred in the external environment.

I think Jesus referred to this when he would say to the recipients of miracles to testify to the world what they had seen. He knew his host was unaware of the miracles at the time they occurred in spacetime, whilst His Higher Self was in Heaven experiencing timelessness. Jesus knew the miracle came from His Higher Self, Christ God, God's Son, and not from His host, the body they called Jesus. Although they occurred because of, and as a consequence of, Jesus's unconditional loving without expectations and in total forgiveness and non-judgement.

So live your life transmuting fear, by not worrying, by keeping calm, continually forgiving away all hurt, pain, temptations and trespasses, earthly thoughts, whilst lovingly, knowingly and trustingly freezing your host's, your body's expectations in the external, in your awareness. Meanwhile your Higher Self in Christ God accepts God's gifts to itself, His and Your miracles, which your host will never have any direct experience or recollection of, or ever expect itself. Still completely in the earthly plane, it places all its trust in Christ God, its Higher Self, to fill and use its beingness with His Holy Spirit for His own Will and purpose.

Chapter 139

Shake it off

"Shake it off" and take "ownership" of your life, whilst at the same moment accepting your true loving nature.

To just rest, to stop judging, there is nothing for us to be but love.

Overlay your love upon all things perceived in your vision.

To just be in our Home in Christ God, with Christ Vision, Loving Vision, healing and correcting what has up till now been poor vision. To place our eternal unconditional loving acceptance upon everything we would look upon, everything God has gifted us.

It is not that there is anything wrong with what God would have us look upon, *the embryonic earth*. He does not judge. It is the attitude we have added to our sight, the attitude of judgement, the stored-up pain, the unforgivenesses of the characters we are not. These are the characters we have adopted from our embryonic past and the cause of our loss of memory of Him and our true Home in Christ God.

We need to shake off their primordial attitude by simple loving acceptance of all God's miraculous gifts, including our embryonic ancestors, their history, and their evolution.

We must make it our purpose each day to want to live in Christ God's Loving Will, our true Home, by continually forgiving away anxieties, not worrying about what transpires in our multiverse or what gifts He would have us look upon, or would take away and make us weep or be angry. Accept all the changes He has introduced and will introduce into your character's life in the present moment. Stop letting thoughts of your past and future take you away from your present moment and enjoyment of His gifts.

You just need to forgive away any hurt, any changes of perception, and trust Him. Overlay your love on all His changes to your life, His gifts in your life.

Accept His perfect grace, His perfect miracles, and behold from within Him, with Christ Vision, Your Heavenly Oneness, our perfect Home, in place of the imperfect world of our embryonic ancestors that we would otherwise witness with our earthly attitude, from the perspective of our adopted characters.

So we need only forgive away all earthly thoughts in our perception, the earthly ideas and temptations of our ghostly shadows streaming into our unguarded minds, by simply accepting them and letting them pass through without attachment, whilst at the same time trusting Our Father's Will for our salvation and an end to the dream of the embryonic earth.

Chapter 140
Remember Gods Love

Remember, everything appearing in your life is exactly as you created it for your learning. So, accept with thanks that you are going through a learning phase of your choosing. Each day is a chosen lesson to endure with forgiveness.

Forgive away any anxiety, pain, suffering, anger, and hate absorbed into your pain body as you witness the embryonic earth in your awareness. Treat each day as starting anew, as if you are going to school to be with your friends. Everyone and everything is a gift from Christ God.

Make your state of mind the sacred altar: light, carefree, wanting to know, happy and joyous, as you accept every original idea from Christ God in its purest and sinless form. Heaven in every stride you take.

Ensure every idea is cleansed and restored after your witnessing before it is returned upon your mind and laid at the altar, the Mind of Christ God.

Remember, it is for you to reveal the miracle behind the façade of the illusion every moment of your day. Create in your awareness the beauty and miraculous version of every idea. It is like borrowing a library book from God's miraculous library, every page, every word perfect and miraculous. You can borrow and view the book, provided you do not tarnish it with any anxieties or fear, worries or pain. The instant you do, it loses its miraculous power, becoming a worthless word salad of no special use.

So remember to cleanse your body and keep your hands clean as you turn each page, free of any anxiety, by continually forgiving away any painful ideas before they become a thought that would dislodge God's words that you would read in your sinless mind.

In summary, in your oneness with Christ and our Father, cleanse your ideas with forgiveness. Restore God's Word, His love, your love and your miraculous gifts, atonement for yourself and your brothers, and the salvation of the world.

Chapter 141

Love attracts Itself

Love attracts itself, and your life is all about attracting love. God's ideas are born from His love.

We experience daily in our lives spoiled versions of His original ideas. His ideas, contaminated by *our* hate, repel each other, causing separation, *the fall of man*, the opposite of oneness.

We must restore God's ideas and oneness with our forgiveness, to allow His love to flow freely, continually, unconditionally and without reservation upon every idea He has gifted.

It is for us to restore His miracles, His original intent, His gifts to our awareness.

In other words, as we go about our lives each day, in every situation, we need only to remember to unconditionally forgive every anxiety and worry, to allow our love to flow into everything and everyone. Thus, ensuring every idea, every gift from God, everything He would have us look upon, is accepted in thankfulness, everything as the miraculous version, the forgiven and restored original idea.

The same ideas, which would otherwise be perceived as the suffering, lacking, wanting version, are the unforgiven ideas that create the embryonic earth and our suffering cosmic ancestors.

This means the thought is what is perceived, created in our awareness by our minds. A miracle is a created, forgiven idea, having been restored or overlaid by love before it enters our mind as a thought.

Every idea is a gift from God. We can choose to overlay the same idea with either love or hate.

It is like living in one of two versions of life. One is the free version, which contains much suffering, unforgiveness and pain. The second is the upgraded version with nothing but joy and happiness.

The price for the upgraded version is to overlay every idea gifted by God with your unconditional forgiveness and love before it enters your mind and becomes a thought, ensuring the miracle is received.

The instant the thought is produced, it is perceived in our awareness.

If the idea enters our mind with love laid upon it (hate cleansed by forgiveness, revealing the love concealed beneath), then you will witness a miracle.

If the idea is left to enter through the back, unguarded door, it will create a thought which will, in our awareness, produce an image of suffering.

Try to live in timeless Heavenly bliss by guarding your mind, ensuring every idea is cleansed with forgiveness, enabling your love to overlay every idea God gives to You before it enters your mind as a thought.

Love will not bond to an idea contaminated by hate. Corrupted ideas must be cleansed first with forgiveness before they can be passed as a loving idea into our minds in order to create miracles.

So live guarding your mind continually with forgiveness, with your love overlaying every idea God gifts to You as you go about your life creating miracles.

Chapter 142
Nothing to do

Remember, every moment there is nothing in the earthly world for your earthly character to do.

So just be who you really are: sinless, resting in being awareness itself, in heavenly peace, without judgement. Rest, treating each day as if you are basking in the light of the Son in the Father, receiving rays of Son-shine, His pure ideas showered upon you and received in purity. Perceive everyone, including yourself, in sinlessness, equally perfect children of God. In sinlessness, create miracles, sense with Christ Vision a world saved. Heavenly ideas, pure without judgement or pain, gently land on your forgiving mind, creating miracles instead of suffering for you and for all mankind.

So, keep anxieties, the clouds of judgement, away with your forgiveness. In Oneness, feel the Son and the Father's heavenly ideas landing on your mind uncorrupted, upon your beautiful mind, on fertile soil, creating beautiful miracles all day long.

If you judge, accept anxieties, you will create the embryonic earth with all its worries and pains in your full awareness, with yourself trapped in the illusionary character you have judged and portray.

So, remember to continually accept and not judge. Acceptance is the opposite of judgement. Forgive away all your judgements of your brother and bask in the light of his sinlessness, the Son of God. In sinlessness, accept His ideas, His gifts, God's reflection, your brothers' gifts, laid gently on your mind as you perceive everyone as equal Sons of God, everyone your brothers.

When you are feeling lost, it is because your awareness is full of your character's earthly judgements, your mind is full of earthly ideas instead of heavenly ideas. The soil has grown weeds where there could be miraculous heavenly fruits, ideas God did not plant. Forgive away the ideas God did not plant and continue to rest in God's living sinlessness as His Son-light continues to shine on you and reflect on your brothers and the world you made.

Acceptance with forgiveness in place of judgement is to draw open the clouds of judgement, to reveal Christ God's ideas in truth, in their original perfect form, creating Heaven here on earth.

Flying with forgiveness and non-earthly judgement is like boarding a powerful rocket ship, cutting through and above the clouds. All the mountains, all the challenges are conquered by your forgiving acceptance and non-judgement, distant memories left far below the clouds, fading out of your mind as you rest in the protection of the Holy Spirit.

So just be, let it all go, and bask in the rays of Son-shine as you journey eternally through the realms of Heaven above the clouds.

Chapter 143
Your hidden torch

Imagine yourself setting off for work on a beautiful sunny morning. During the day, whilst driving home, heavy clouds build up, and soon after dusk descends it is pitch black with seemingly impenetrable dark clouds, with no starlight and no moonlight. Every light source is hidden from you. Your headlights are no longer working, and you are forced to stop and rethink. You are desperate, frustrated, frightened, unable even to see your hand in front of your face.

Hours later, still in darkness, sobbing and praying, you ask God to help you find your way home. You look and find a small torch hidden under your car seat, not very powerful but nonetheless bright enough to reflect off objects directly in front of you, such that you can carry on with your journey home. You step out of the car and begin to walk.

As you do, you start to pass signposts directing you towards your home, each printed on highly reflective surfaces, bright and clear. You notice that as your mind focuses more and more on the surfaces of each object you pass, even the plants, trees, and animals crossing your path, everything has a reflective surface. Your torch easily picks out each object, ensuring your safe return home.

Imagine the torch in your pocket is forgiveness, and its light is your love, your *magic dust*. The surfaces reflecting your light are opportunities to increase your faith, to increase your *magic dust*, and to inform you how much faith you have left — a measure of how much you forgive and how much love you shine on each object. With Christ Vision, everything and everyone you look at is lit up by your love, your torch of forgiveness, and the love reflected back at you is increased, making yourself the light on the hill brighter, lighting up the sky, everyone, and the whole world surrounding you.

So treat everything and everyone as an opportunity to increase your faith and brighten your light. Do not judge, do not discriminate. Forgive and accept everyone and everything. If you discriminate, if you doubt, both your light and your faith are diminished.

So, everything in your multiverse is a God-given gift to increase your faith as you forgive and polish the reflective surface of everyone and everything with your forgiveness. Remove any anxieties and worries to witness your love reflecting back upon yourself brighter, continually reigniting your flame, your light, your faith growing stronger and brighter.

You see, over the millennia, we have lost our faith, as faith is the product of forgiveness and love. Hate has been allowed to grow in our unguarded and separated minds. We have done so through our knowing of the earth, the embryonic earth, knowing of good and evil, of how our ancestors came to be. Like them, by constantly judging and not forgiving, we have forgotten how to love.

It is like using up almost all the magic dust God built into our beingness, His children, His creation, and not knowing we could always have made an infinite amount more. So much more, so easily, by forgiving, not judging, and instead loving all His creations.

When you place forgiveness with your love, the product is faith. Faith is your light, and it increases and increases because the two multiply with one another each time they meet, eventually increasing exponentially.

So, in summary, continually forgive, do not judge, and love all things in your multiverse. Do not judge as you forgive, and multiply your faith to reach Christ Vision, your destiny cloaked in the protection of the Holy Spirit.

Chapter 144

Reborn into Christ hood

In the last living moments of the ego, as it approaches its final end, in that moment it fully understands that as it dies it will be reborn in Christ, to live and serve mankind's salvation.

Its human form it gladly relinquishes to Christ Itself to use, as Christ and *Itself* adopt its last dying wish and common purpose, which is to shine Christ's ever-expanding, fully encompassing, loving light and forgiveness upon all of mankind, upon every Creative Idea God gifts to His Son and all of His Children that return to Him, their brother.

So, remember to rest and be in peace. Rest in your beingness in Christ.

Do not judge, accept and treat everything and everyone as an opportunity to serve Christ in your common purpose with Him, to increase your faith and the faith of all mankind, as they and all of His creation rejoice in your resurrection.

So, extend His Son-Light, reflecting His and your loving forgiveness, your common purpose, upon all things in your multiverse, as everything and everyone are lit up and seen and known to you in Christ Vision as your teacher, your student and your saviour.

Chapter 145

Take refuge under blue skies

If the ego chooses to die then no earthly thoughts, no earthly emotions, no earthly desires or temptations remain. In other words, the ego places its full trust with Christ God, or it convinces its body to jump off a cliff, or something like that!

The ego's last act is to put its trust in something seemingly invisible to all the ego's bodily senses. To trust Christ God to provide for its safety, to satisfy all its fears. To, in fact, step aside entirely and be known no more. To set aside its own will and let go of the pendulum of time and all earthly laws.

It is the constant stream of thoughts landing on your mind, creating all the temptations that imprison you to the earth you create and to your ego. Imagine an old-fashioned pendulum clock swinging back and forth, powered by every earthly thought your mind accepts and every associated temptation you crave.

As long as you follow these thoughts and temptations, you will always be trapped in earth time and earth laws.

Think of earthly thoughts and temptations as the energy keeping the momentum going on the pendulum. Your ego clings to the pendulum, to temptations, swinging back and forth from one earthly temptation to another, keeping time going, leaving you stuck and going nowhere.

To break free, all you have to do, and it is not really doing anything other than being your true self, is to guard your mind. Guard it from earthly judgements and forgive away any pain, any anxieties you have been clinging to. Take away the energy from the pendulum, feeding the ego, keeping it alive. Starve the ego by not judging and forgiving away its pain body and eventually it will cease to exist. Time, its creation, will stop with its demise, along with the earthly laws, allowing your awareness to live in the present, in Oneness with Christ Vision in Christ God.

So, try to remember during your day not to worry about anything you witness, and that you are not subjected to any laws on earth or time. Earthly laws and time are your ego's creation, and they are not you.

Create a gap between you and all the earthly laws, and stop the pendulum in your life by letting go of it and trusting God will catch you.

So, detach from earthly thoughts and temptations and break away from time into stillness and peace by simply letting your forgiveness and love without judgement unconditionally shine and reflect back on you from everything you create.

Resist temptation and pause time. Pause the earthly laws by allowing your true self in Christ, withholding judgement with Christ

Vision, beholding His miracles transforming your world as your mind is one again with Christ's Shared Thoughts with the Father, to make the perfect version of everything you would look upon and create.

You see, the earth needs you to be tempted to exist in the imperfect form it appears.

So, remember, everything in your multiverse is there because you created it in your mind, with the earthly thoughts your mind accepted. The decision will always remain with your mind to purify your thoughts, to pause the laws of earth and time by guarding your mind from receiving any more judgements. Non-judgement is to reject the laws of earth and time.

This is why, on a beautiful warm spring day, as you rest looking up at blue skies, everything perfect, your mind satisfied, time seems to stop. You appear to have everything you need, and you wish the moment would last forever. That thought is judgement, is a creation of an unforgiven fear. It opens the floodgates of more thoughts and the moment, the instant you felt everything perfect, is lost.

The purpose of forgiveness is to expel any anxieties, emotions and pain you have accumulated in your pain body and to rid yourself of all the thoughts that would spoil that perfect spring morning instant of timelessness. So rid yourself of all the pain, all the demons, with forgiveness, and guard your mind from further judgements, earthly invasions, and behold your heavenly creation's rejuvenation in Christ God with Christ Vision, your new way of seeing and knowing, in loving peace without judgement.

Give thanks, love, and forgive your creation, and be tempted no more. Take a break from knowing of your cosmic ancestors and know them through the eyes of your Creator with Christ Vision.

Remember, everything is temptation and possesses the power to imprison your mind and fill it with earthly thoughts. Everything is bait, nothing is exempt, and everything and everyone, including your loved ones, is designed to keep you baited, locked into the embryonic earth, lost in temptation, with your mind working overtime as it is constantly distracted with a barrage of more earthly thoughts and judgements.

Imagine an octopus with an unlimited number of legs. It only needs one of those legs to latch on to one of your judged creations for you to become a prisoner.

So, resist temptation, work on severing every attachment, every judgement. Practise fasting, create and maintain space and a gap between your mind and the invasive thoughts and temptations, like the firebreaks designed into a managed forest.

If you are being tempted, remember you are being tempted and do not judge. Judgements have an infinite number of legs too, and will keep you attached just as food, alcohol, people, lovers, a cup of coffee and so on would do. Everything you manifest in your world has the potential to be an attachment when you judge. Metaphorically, this is the devil, your jailor.

So, practise being independent of earthly temptations and continue to forgive, accept and love all you create without judgement. Be the observer and not what is being observed.

Live giving thanks to God your Father for the opportunity not only to observe our cosmic ancestors, but also to live amongst them, to thank them by being them, by temporarily adopting their fears, hopes and dreams, and teaching us how to increase our faith. As we, like them, take strength from their memory, with courage, like them, continuing to forgive and love at every opportunity, we increase our loving light, accepting from God His faith in us as we leave their world with our exponentially increasing loving acceptance and forgiveness.

So, treat each moment of each day as an opportunity, a gift, to forgive away with loving acceptance and without judgement the sin that fear would have you see with earthly vision, as you witness miracles instead, seen with your restored Christ Vision.

Chapter 146

VCR goggles and headphones

How does it feel from our perspective (the lost, the sinners, those trapped by temptations), as we are about to enter into Oneness with our Creator? To enter into His peace, happiness and joy, when you are so close that we can almost feel it.

It is like worrying about being in Heaven when you are already in Heaven but with your head covered with VCR goggles and headphones, able to reach out and touch whilst at the same time living out a fearful nightmare. All you have to do is take off the blindfold and the earplugs and know you are already in Heaven.

It is completely insane!

So, each day, calm your beingness. Do not worry about not feeling happy and wanting to be elsewhere, including Heaven. Instead, simply open your eyes and ears and see the perfect version instead of what you are already aware of. Reset yourself, your beingness, to the default mode: seeing without judgement and relinquishing your anxieties and all your pain body with forgiveness.

See yourself once again as you were created and still are, by detaching from the fearful images, from the fear of everyone and everything around you, by simply guarding your mind from earthly judgements, and letting your shining acceptance, gratitude, love and forgiveness illuminate instead everything, reflect off everything and everyone in your multiverse, in your awareness. Lighting up where you have always been. Gift to yourself and your world the unlimited miracles that you, in Christ God, have in store.

No longer accept your fearful versions of God's ideas. Gift to yourself the perfect versions of every God-given gift your fearful, unsolicited earthly thoughts would hide from you.

Chapter 147

Call upon your true self

To call upon God is to call upon your true self, to call upon the Oneness who is you in Christ God, the Christ within you, uncorrupted by earthly thoughts, the sinless version of yourself.

To call upon the Christ within is to shield against earthly thoughts.

Miracles are witnessed in your awareness when your ego knowingly, unconditionally forgives, fore-gives-away earthly judgements. This allows your love, Christ God's Love, to reflect upon everything, God's original perfect idea restored, replacing the corrupted version.

Your unconditional loving forgiveness lights up everything, everybody, and everything seen in its miraculous version.

Remember that you are the torch that lights up the darkness of your multiverse. Only you have the power to do that, to see your world in the loving light of forgiveness, accepting everything and everyone without judgement in their perfect form.

Everything and everyone glows brighter as your faith grows stronger and stronger, as you relinquish more and more fear and judgement, diminishing your anxieties and pain body with more and more forgiveness, and reflecting your light on more and more of God's original ideas. Your name and His are becoming more and more as One, as your will is His Will, One Will.

In other words, your goal is to accept the purest, uncorrupted Godly thoughts only.

Remember, earthly thoughts and earthly judgements dilute and corrupt God's word, His original ideas. It is like putting the wrong fuel into a rocket ship. The fuel is so useless that you can barely leave the ground and escape your world's expectations.

So, break free from earthly ideas and dwell in our Father's Heavenly Ideas, in His Heavenly orbit with your faith, maintaining your Heavenly journey.

Reject the pull of earthly thoughts, earthly temptations and judgements that would imprison you, everyone and everything in a self-imposed exile in hell.

Live using the correct fuel: uncorrupted, undiluted fuel, free of fear, anxiety, judgement and unforgiveness.

So, do not judge, do not accept any more earthly thoughts contaminating your mind, and know your true power, God's ideas, His strength, whilst continually guarding against any further contamination, anxiety and pain that would diminish your faith.

With Christ Vision, see through the clouds of judgement with your unconditional loving forgiveness and acceptance, lifting the veil that obscures where you have always been.

Jesus taught: *"Man cannot live by bread alone,"* but needs every word from God our Father. In other words, to really live as God intended, He has made available for all time His original ideas, His original every word, to replenish our strength so that we may live in permanent happiness and joy.

So, increase your faith, shine your loving forgiveness and acceptance without judgement on your world, and hear God's Voice transforming your world into Heaven.

Remember, it is forgiving the pain away rather than the sin. The sin is done, it is past. When the healing is done, you will find your unconditional peace and love flowing through you into your world, rather than the memory and horror of the event, of any tragedy or any sin, no matter how evil. Every perception can be transformed this way. Forgiving away the pain is to let your love wash away the post-event memory and nightmare that would otherwise stain your life and prevent you from living in faith.

Chapter 148

The elephant in the room

As you know them, unconditionally forgive your brother, your sister, everyone you meet, even your enemy. Forgive everyone, including yourself.

You cannot know your true self unless you cease judging others.

You are the elephant in the room, the creator of everything you witness. So, if you do not want more suffering, do not judge, and forgive away thoughts of suffering for you, your brother, everyone.

If you want only Heavenly peace and joy, simply do not judge and create what you want from love. Accept your gifts of Heavenly love and joy upon yourself when you see everyone and everything in sinlessness, in Christ Vision.

You are the devil of your multiverse, your world, when you judge, creating hell on earth.

You are Christ God, the Saviour of your world, when you rid yourself of earthly judgements and allow forgiveness and love to replace anxiety, worries, fears and hate, and let your love shine upon everything and everyone, reflecting back on you.

So, take ownership of your world. Nothing happens to you. You are the Self, the witness, creating what you witness. Forgiveness gives you the power to forgive away your pain body and the thoughts it creates, the thoughts you do not want, the things you do not want to create, and to accept loving, creative thoughts in their place, God's shared thoughts upon your mind, and to witness.

Accept your true self in Christhood and know your Father and Christ God in you.

In summary, despite how frightening and fearful, know everything and everyone in sinlessness. Only then will you be reunified with our Father, everything and everyone in Heavenly Love, bringing salvation to the entire world, your world, and seeing your face reflected back at you in Christ God Vision.

Chapter 149

Myself in Christ God is everything

In other words, I am nothing, my ego, yet my Self in Christ God is everything.

From the standpoint of a non-existent or greatly diminished ego that understands that it-self, at best a ghost, is no-thing, nothing at all, the only Self that really exists is Christ God, the Holy Ghost, the witness of the whole world, your true Self, manifesting in the ego's awareness by faith and faith alone.

The Holy Ghost is the only Self that can remember everything, hold every truth, every gift provided by its Creator, in its original perfect form, in its mind.

It is like saying the ego has finally realised it is really spirit trapped in a human ghostly form. In a ghostly world, it never in reality belonged. The same feeling we all have lived with, a sense of not belonging. The ego's understanding that it never existed in physical reality, ever in the history of the cosmos. As if life itself, consciousness, had played a trick of sorts upon it. Yet the trick became reality in the birth of the Son of God, God's perfect gift to mankind, God's belief that mankind was deserving of becoming His

Son, through whom all of us could live eternally as one mind in Him, in Christ God, forever gifted every perfect gift in their purest, original and most sinless and perfect form.

It is like God, in the form of one of His angels, breathed into Pinocchio declaring to all His children: from now on, you will be one of my many real children living fearlessly, joyfully within MySelf eternally.

Yet in reality, in the embryonic earth, as then each living entity that ever lived, its essence, as each creature and human died, every ghostly egoic essence and every memory that ever lived was harvested by angels and added to the book of truth.

Do not worry about the fearful world and circumstances you find yourself in. Instead, rest, want to know without judgement. Want to remember everything in perfect sinlessness, as God's perfect original Idea, including Yourself, your perfect True Self. Continually resting in God's Love, lovingly, forgivingly knowing without judging yourself, the Holy Spirit living in all things, including all your brothers.

In other words, forgive and love YourSelf by indiscriminately not judging all things, forgiving away your pain body, enjoying all God's Gifts to You, His Child.

Rest in being in your Holy Spirit, silently living and breathing in everything and everyone, as you accept gratefully each of God's Gifts to You without earthly judgements.

It is upon you to take ownership of your world, receive it, bless it and transform it from earthly hell to perfect Heaven by not contaminating God's original Ideas with earthly judgements landing on your mind.

So remember, through total forgiveness, forgive away every anxiety, every pain you carry, and filter every earthly judgement from your mind, leaving only God's original perfect ideas to create the Heaven and salvation you seek for your world.

Chapter 150

Laugh at judgement

Remember to laugh at judgement, to think it could hold you prisoner. You, God's Holy Son, cannot be bound.

Remember to laugh at judgement and shine your loving faith on everyone you meet and set them free from the prison you once shared.

Remember to see with Christ Vision, to look past judgement and through the veil of sin as if it were a thick dark fog hiding your Heavenly truth beyond, lit up by the torch of your loving and shining faith, reflecting off every surface, every brother, everyone, every friend and every enemy. Everyone and everything, living and non-living, all known to you and each other in sinlessness, in Christ Vision.

So, remember today to continually and unconditionally forgive and love without judgement all of your creation and reveal miracles in place of sin, transforming your former earthly prison into Heaven for you and all mankind.

Chapter 151

Taming the Rays

The great play of life. It is what we see as the embryonic earth is revealed to us each day and each lifetime. The great light show.

The great Rays can be thought of, I suppose, as beamed to us in the form of light energy and received by us *untamed* and *unfiltered*, like a wild, beautiful stallion which requires us, God's Children, all the Sons of God, all our brothers, to learn how to accept and ride in peace and joyfulness.

In other words, rather than trying and failing to get on, or being thrashed around like you are riding a bucking bronco only to fall off again and again, we must all learn to ride the beast majestically and gracefully, all God's children riding side by side within Him, God our Creator.

So, the great Rays, the great play of life, must be tamed, must be filtered to purity, brought to stillness within your beingness, by forgiveness, by forgiving all things, by blessing it, blessing all things, loving it, loving everyone and everything.

This is equivalent to you, God's Son, calmly, with courage, approaching and taking ownership of the beast, taking ownership of your life, your beautiful gift from our Heavenly Father. So, approach your life with continual forgiveness. Do not allow the pain body to form, do not allow judgements to infest your mind. Be gentle in your beingness, showing it tenderness and loving care as you peacefully, gently, majestically commence your journey through Heavenly Life with all your siblings and your Creator in your own salvation and that of all men.

Chapter 152
Warp speed ahead

Now imagine the great Rays once again. Imagine you now set the great Rays to warp speed. Made possible with your unconditional loving forgiveness upon the great Rays, upon the play of life, upon your multiverse, upon your life, no longer fearful, no longer tempted. All anxieties, fears and pain instantly repelled by your forgiveness.

In other words, you have mastered how to surf the great Rays, how to surf life, and paradise, Heaven, is now all around you. You have *telly-ported* (excuse the pun) into pure sinless beingness, and all around you, you see in Christ Vision everything created in shared Thoughts with our God.

You have climbed up the slippery slide of life, and now you have slid down at warp speed and arrived back home.

With forgiveness as your engine fuel, your Heavenly fuel, you no longer keep looking sideways. No longer are you distracted by fear and temptations. Your body is light, you carry no pain, and your mind is still, with no more judgements and filled with God's perfect thoughts only. Your view is unobstructed, looking straight ahead, and all around is your Heavenly home. All of mankind have disembarked after having boarded your spaceship with you, everyone having landed on Heaven's beautiful shores with you, their captain.

So, I guess this earthly life is all about preparing us to really start living in what many term *the great leap of faith*. Not looking back or sideways anymore, but forgivingly, without judgement, trustingly, lovingly letting go of all attachments, no longer gripping the walls you built and giving yourself permission to just be, to rest where you always were, bathing where you started your journey, in the crystal waters of our Creator's Ocean of Love.

Chapter 153

The Octopus and the drain pipe

In order to understand, you need to teach yourself. The more we teach ourselves, in sincerity, without fear and without judgement, that which we really believe, with forgiveness as our compass, the closer to God's Truth we find ourselves. At the same time, we live joyously in Him.

It is with these thoughts that you should imagine your ego as an octopus stuck in a drainpipe, trying desperately to survive whilst grasping at the pipe walls.

It was accidentally flushed into the pipe when it was a tiny baby. It learnt to survive of sorts, feeding on the sludge of the pipe walls without any knowledge or memory of the ocean, its true home.

One day, it decides it has to get out of the pipe. It has outgrown the pipe and is stuck, fearing death, thinking it will die and feeling claustrophobic. It is trapped against the pipe walls, unable to move, desperate, telling itself it is time to escape its situation.

Then it discovers that if it stops feeding on the sludge sticking to the pipe walls, it gets smaller and once again can move in the pipe. It quickly learns that the less it feeds on the sticky walls, the faster it slides. After letting go completely and no longer being addicted to feeding on the pipe walls, in no time at all it finds itself swimming in a beautiful, perfect lagoon, in paradise with all its family.

And so it is for us. We have created this false self, brainwashed by a constant stream of judgements, thoughts and temptations. It has allowed these to settle in its mind, with a pain body so big it is frightened to look.

It is time to just be. Our Father has already gifted us Paradise. We need only to open our eyes and see it is all around us. It needs no thoughts of judgement. So, forgive away every pain, everything you carry, all the anger, all the painful memories you cling to and all the addictions your ego feeds on, the ghosts that fill your mind. Guard your mind, and just be. Know everything in Christ Vision, in your true self, and know Heaven in Oneness with Christ God, our Creator.

Chapter 154

The spinning electron

It seems it was God's plan from the beginning that learning be instantly available to each and every one from the source of truth, our Creator Himself.

The quality of what we teach and study depends on our sinlessness. If you learn and your mind is cleared of sinful thoughts in other words, your mind is cleared one hundred per cent of earthly, fear-driven thoughts then your learning will be instant. Teacher and pupil learn simultaneously. We are using our energy to teach ourselves efficiently. Rather than worrying about time, we get to choose the speed and the way we want to progress our spiritual awakening. In other words, how much we are prepared to wander in and out of sin, in and out of pure sinlessness, in and out of earthly fears.

There are various levels or planes of evolution of the mind, taught in many different forms all around the world. Our purpose has always been to climb the ladder of knowledge, the various planes so to speak, and when the learning mechanism itself is fully understood it can be climbed infinitely more efficiently and eventually everything will be known instantly.

Essentially, every page in the book of life is available to us right now. God is the library, the source of all knowledge, and we in Him can accelerate our learning much faster if we escape the earthly chains of fear, judgement and temptation. In other words, if we can escape sin and choose to supercharge our progression in sinlessness, without judgement.

When we look up the ladder in this clean state of mind, we find it is attached to a rescue helicopter of sorts that places our beingness instantly at the top of the highest mountain where every page is seen and all truth is revealed as we accept all the gifts that salvation in Oneness provides.

So make it your intention not to judge anything our Creator reveals in your multiverse, and supercharge your learning. Stop holding your learning back, stop reading the same page over and over again the same page you feel most comfortable with. Teach yourself, the pupil, His pupil in His Oneness, everything He would have you know.

Pray that God gives you the strength to be more attentive to His voice, to unconditionally forgive all your anxieties, fears and pains, and to not judge what He would reveal so you do not stumble. See your brother and everyone in sinlessness in the Heavenly realm, all of us listening to His voice, unconditionally forgiving and not judging what He would reveal.

The source of all obstacles to truth is the fear of death. All judgements are thoughts reinforcing your fear of death. Judgements are essentially running rings around you every moment of your life, so fast they seem to create a cloud of fear that imprisons you behind a dark veil.

Imagine then that something is running around you with you at its centre. It moves so fast it is like an electron spinning around an atom invisible, yet seemingly an object all the same. Something always seemingly threatening your existence, the cause of all your unhappiness, creating a veil, an invisible wall of fear behind which you are brainwashed by your ego, a seeming ruler at the centre of your beingness. You dare not look past the veil. Your awareness dares not try and step through the veil. It chooses to hide behind the veil, to bury itself like a mole in the darkness.

So practise stopping the judgement, stand guard over your sacred mind, and eventually you will stop the fear of death. Continually know with certainty that you cannot die. You are eternal awareness itself, always at the centre of your multiverse.

Stop the electron from spinning, stop the judgement, and the veil is no more. All God's gifts, all your gifts to yourself in His Oneness, will be revealed, which your ego has kept masked behind its wall of judgement.

The ego is a force of evolution. It is a creation of evolutionary nature. It vibrates in all living things to keep them alive in what was the embryonic earth, where mankind originally evolved.

You see, we are in reality already at the top of the evolutionary ladder, at the top of the levels of evolution. We are at the top of the seven planes, or any number you choose depending upon which part of the world or what belief you subscribe to. Our species evolved into Christ God, the pinnacle of evolution which you can witness in your awareness right now as you become one with Christ God's Oneness, as you bring to an end all judgements and unforgiveness.

So stop running away from death. You can never die. God created your awareness indestructible. Let your light burst through the veil you created and light up your entire multiverse.

Everything and everyone's embryonic memory past and future is preserved, alive and accessible in Christ God right now.

When you have stopped worrying about your own death and the death of everything and everyone, you know eternal life in Christ God with Christ Vision. All knowledge, past and future, is available to you in an instant if you want it. All you have to do to access this range of vision is rest and be yourself in the awareness that you are.

If fear comes knocking on your door, simply shine the light of your awareness on the judgement and transmute the anxiety and fear with your acceptance and loving forgiveness. Your loving forgiveness is your divine power, your magic dust to turn any scary moment into a safe and secure moment. Your emotional state determines the form of the ghostly, illusionary apparitions in your multiverse.

Acceptance, courage and loving forgiveness are what Daniel invoked when faced with a savage hungry lion, turning the moment into a warm, loving experience as the beast lay down by his side, offering him protection as the Holy Spirit cloaked him and the lion.

So it is with all things: conquer your fear of death in all situations. Fear not a stranger or an enemy; love him, forgive him as you would forgive and love your own child, and watch your multiverse be transformed from fear and flight, by your loving acceptance, into Heaven and divine beauty.

Chapter 155

Seeing Holiness all around

The whole purpose of learning is to realise our fullest potential.

Journeying home is just a metaphor for reaching our *Heavenly source.* Our *Heavenly source* is again another metaphor for our final goal, which is to restore Christ Vision to our sight with our awareness cloaked in the Holy Spirit, having chosen and succeeded in ending our separation from Oneness with our Creator.

Your journey home is like driving a vehicle initially in darkness.

Not worrying and forgiving away any and all anxieties and pains you carry, letting go of every cruelty we have witnessed, is like releasing the handbrake and unhitching a heavy trailer you have been towing.

Driving forward with your lights continually switched on during the day and night, through good and bad weather, is like forgivingly and lovingly wanting to know your multiverse, each other, and your whole world with unconditional forgiveness and love, without attaching to anxieties, judgements and pain.

Judging is like braking and slowing down or going in the opposite direction, the wrong direction.

Temptations can be like useless detours, taking bumpy lanes through hostile, rough terrain.

When you see in Christ Vision, you see yourself in all things, with all things seeing you, all things worshipping you, their Creator, in your Home, your Kingdom.

God made us perfect and in Himself, not just in His Image or likeness or separate to Himself, which your fearful ego would have you believe, but actually in Him where you not only have all His attributes as His Child but also remembrance of what He created, what everything ever was or was ever created by Him during the zillions upon zillions of eons of timelessness.

So, when you see yourself and all you see looking back at you in sinlessness, then you are witnessing in Christ Vision, in Christ God Vision, in God Vision, seeing everything you created Holy, whole and in sinlessness without judgement and totally forgiven. You are finally seeing your Heavenly Home.

This day I will strive not to judge my brother, and so will not judge myself nor my Creator. I will strive to forgive away all the pain of separation, the pain that would have me believing I am small, worthless and fragile.

Instead, I will strive to see truth with Christ Vision. Everything, all I create, I will see in holiness and sinlessness, everything looking back at me in loving worship as I, without judgement, allow only love to fill my eyes and my whole beingness as I worship everything surrounding me, transformed by my Holiness.

Chapter 156

The Scram Engine

There appear to be two ways of seeing:

Seemingly normal human perception

Or

Christ God Vision, where trust, tolerance, honesty, forgiveness and non-judgement seem to shield you as the Holy Spirit is invoked.

The Holy Spirit, the highest evolutionary form of mankind, creates everything for you to see in Christ Vision, to see in truth.

Earth man, a physical, fragile body and prisoner of what its ego perceives, is full of judgement, anger, lack of tolerance, dishonesty, lack of trust and acceptance, defensive, full of constant frustrations and doubts, in constant fear, a mind in turmoil.

Filled with the Holy Spirit, your true self sees in truth, with loving trust, forgiveness, acceptance, tolerance, in defenselessness, non-judgement and a mind at peace.

So, each moment of your day, do not worry about anything at all, even salvation itself, and submit to Your Higher Self's Will. Be one with God's Will, seeing with Christ Vision, shielded by the

Holy Spirit, invoked by the ideals you live by: trust, forgiveness, in defenselessness, tolerance, honesty and acceptance.

Practise seeing our ancestors as yourself in Christ God's Vision by accepting and simultaneously forgiving away their pain you feel as you are them.

Enemy or friend, see them without judgement, with love replacing fear always, trustingly, in defenselessness, freeing them and yourselves from the chains of suffering and want, having expelled every last pain you carry for them, bringing salvation to them and filling them with the Holy Spirit.

Each day, wake up with a positive attitude, knowing in your heart that you will iron out the last few creases of your life, knowing the last page is almost written for you, at which point you can hand your work to your teacher, saying in honesty, "Lord, this is my life's work complete," expecting nothing in return whilst receiving everything He has to give.

With your unlimited courage, do not be afraid to look upon the embryonic earth, your home, seeing it in heavenly perfection and know perfect beingness, stillness and eternal peace.

Like some futuristic scram engine aircraft, let forgiveness, trust, tolerance, honesty and non-judgement power your life through your multiverse.

Do not worry about thinking about salvation either. Simply move through life like a scram engine without sticking to temptations or judgements. Remain detached as you fly higher and higher in joy and happiness, simply aware of everything without worrying.

Temptation is like passing through the embryonic earth on a travellator at the greatest museum built by God.

Each time you are fearful, tempted and pass judgement, you step off the travellator and your awareness becomes engrossed, obsessed and imprisoned by what it is you are experiencing.

A seeming illusion where you are living in an ancient world, playing out one of the ancient characters, experiencing what appears to be yourself (the ego) in a seemingly real world surrounding you everywhere.

So continually, unconditionally, acceptingly, forgivingly, not judgingly, lovingly remain detached and shine your loving Heavenly light in tranquil peace. In timelessness let every moment remain still, as if the travellator of ancient illusionary living has stopped and in an instant everything, every exhibit in the embryonic earth is changed miraculously by yourself and filled by the Holy Spirit into a perfect Heavenly version of what it was.

This is perhaps why some men and women become warriors instead of soldiers. As they engage in battle, sword to sword, their shield is the Holy Spirit as they fight their enemies, converting their fears instantly into courage, with forgiveness, without judging, without temptation and hate.

Or perhaps why, in recordings captured by CCTV, we see time and time again images of individuals escaping seemingly certain death as disaster occurs all around them.

Chapter 157

Your Mind the Gateway to God

Feel safe and happy. God is in all things. So lovingly accept God as your multiverse as you accept Him in everything and everyone your thoughts perceive, friend or enemy, family or strangers, humans or animals. He is everything and everywhere in you and me. He is omniscient and omnipresent.

So be kind, gentle and trusting of all things and everyone. It is God and yourself to whom you are kind, trusting and gentle. You are God's child, whole in Him always. You are Holy as He is Holy. You are Whole as He is Whole.

Faithfulness is unwavering determination to keep your mind clear for God's ideas to land and create in your multiverse. It is trusting in defenselessness that God's ideas are worth infinitely more than the ego's thoughts, landing and filling your unguarded mind.

So it is you can achieve one hundred per cent faithfulness when you guard your mind one hundred per cent from earthly thoughts, filling it with embryonic earthly illusions.

So, each moment, be one hundred per cent faithful to God's thoughts, rest in forgiveness, keeping your mind clear for His thoughts to create the gifts He would bestow on you and all mankind.

Remember always: your mind is a gateway for God's love to flow into the hearts of all mankind, bringing salvation to everything and everyone. So remember to see God in all things, where you will find there is you looking back at yourself. Forgive, do not judge, accept and love your brothers and enemies equally.

Let the Holy Spirit fill you, and see within them God and yourself looking back at you. See you looking back at you. Everything and everywhere is God, is yourself, looking back at you in what is Oneness.

Chapter 158

Unclog your Mind

The only way to salvation is through forgiveness of all the earthly ideas that would clog your mind and prevent your open-mindedness to our Creator's ideas.

So it is, we need only forgive away earthly, worrisome thoughts, creating space in our minds and opening our minds to God's ideas to land, which never fail in applying the correction, the perfect version, the perfect outcome.

Remember throughout your day to forgive away your fears and worries, no matter how bad or frightening they are. Give everything away and let God's thoughts create in your mind.

In other words, worrying and your worries will prevent the Holy Spirit from adjusting your path, ironing out the poor outcomes needed to make your journey easier.

Chapter 159
Created in His Likeness

Remember this about yourself always: when you forgive others, you forgive yourself. When you give to others, you give to yourself. When you offer kindness to others, you offer kindness to yourself. When you do not judge others, you do not judge yourself. And as you judge others, you judge yourself.

As you love others, you love yourself.

You are everyone and everything, created in His likeness, created in His Oneness.

Chapter 160

Heal yourself

Salvation is about being the real you. Salvation is healing yourself, and it is a decision a decision to remember to be the real you.

So, make the decision that you have had enough of the earthly illusion and wake up to who you and your brothers have always been.

Forgiveness gives you the ability to detach and, with practice, unglue yourself and others from the illusion. It allows you to unglue yourself from your pain body, from feelings of guilt for things you think you have done.

You have done nothing. You have committed no crimes. Do not judge yourself. Judging yourself and others is another form of earthly temptation designed to shackle you to the illusion of the embryonic earth.

You are the witness of your host and all mankind. You are present in all things in your multiverse as a witness only. You have never been a participant. You have never committed or conspired to anything you have witnessed.

Witnessing all things, you are as sinless now as the instant you were created. You are sinless. Through forgiveness, remember who and what you are. You are God's sinless child, one in Him, one in His Holy Spirit.

Break free and no longer identify yourself with what you think is your pain body, the earthly thoughts and temptations of your host. All these things are designed to imprison your host, such that it continues to know of the embryonic earth, our cosmic ancestors and of the good and evil they evolved through.

Accept that what you have experienced was designed to fool your host but not you. Be fooled no longer. You are not your host. None of it is real for your Holy Spirit. Break free completely and just be yourself, free from temptations, one in the Holy Spirit.

The real you lives in the Oneness of the Holy Spirit.

Chapter 161
Living in Brilliance

Let depression be a warning to you that you have let your guard down to your mind. Make it your decision once again to correct your mind, to guard it from earthly thoughts, doubts and judgements, and to find refuge again in sinlessness, in the peace of the Holy Spirit.

Remember, salvation is a decision. A decision to forgive away all earthly doubts and judgements and deny the creation of the imposter, the substitution of you by an ego that is not real, and the creation of the imperfect illusion that you think is your world and multiverse.

So today, breathe in and make an affirmation: *Holy Spirit, fill me as Your will. In You alone is my rest assured. In God's Thoughts alone is salvation's healing a reality for everyone and everything. I seek Your vision, Christ God Vision.*

Make it your decision to be filled with your Holy Spirit throughout the day as you forgive away invasive worries. Forgive away the doubts and judgements you would accept and manifest in your multiverse, the doubts that would lead you to imaginary sickness for yourself and those you created around you.

Let your faith, the absence of your doubts and judgements, bring peace and healing and remembrance within them and yourself, whereupon they will call you brother and so deny themselves no longer, as they see themselves in you as you do in them.

Remember, living in brilliance is living in the Holy Spirit.

It is getting onto the great stage of life after having overcome stage fright. It is stepping up to the next level of evolution of our beingness. It is leaving behind the earthly thought streams you became used to, after trading them for God's thoughts and the creation of the perfect version of your world.

Depression is like stepping off the stage without a plan, without a strategy. So, make it your strategy, your decision every minute of the day to forgive away the devilish thoughts, the deep-seated fears that would bring you down.

Guard your mind. Purify your mind. Let it be your decision to let only God's sinless thoughts land in your mind, creating your perfect multiverse and filling it with brilliance, the Holy Spirit, for all eternity in you, your brothers and the whole world.

Chapter 162
Hearing Gods Voice

The giving up of judgement, the prerequisite for hearing God's Voice.

The reason we appear to be lost in our illusionary world is simply because we do not hear, we do not listen for God's silent thoughts while we are too busy judging. Only when our minds are silent do God's thoughts create in our lives the miracles we yearn for.

All we need to do, and it is a big "all", is filter the ideas landing in our minds that will determine the outcome of our day.

In other words, our thoughts create everything we perceive. The ideas we accept into our minds create the thoughts and are the cause of all our perceptions.

If we continually filter, selectively, the ideas landing in our minds — in other words, make judgements for each and every one of those thoughts — we would simply go mad, running around in constant circles thinking, *this is the answer to my salvation, my problems*, and the following week, *this is the answer*, and so on.

The truth is the needle in the haystack of ideas. It is the one idea, the golden needle, God's idea and thought. The one key, the one thought that alone contains all of salvation, the narrow door to your freedom.

So, remember every day, every hour and minute, to live in God's ideas by simply filtering away from your mind, forgiving away every anxiety and every pain in your pain body, everything forgiven away except God's ideas and thoughts.

Guard your mind. Guard your sanctuary, and you will find rest eternally in God's Son, in Him, in the true you, in the Oneness of the Father and the Son in your Holy Spirit.

So, do not worry or care about anything you witness on your journey to get there. The illusionary mirages will eventually fade out as surely as the earthly thoughts in your mind, which with practice will no longer haunt you.

So, each moment, strive to live as a child, living each day in sinlessness, in innocence, in defenselessness, trusting in unconditional forgiveness, knowing your faith in God's idea will shield you, as your courage will guard and protect your mind from earthly thoughts and temptations.

Chapter 163

Your judgements are your prison walls

Our heavenly freedom is gained when we do not judge. So remember, when confused or feeling emotionally out of integrity, you have yet again lost your mind to earthly thoughts of ingratitude, temptations and judgements, creating your illusionary, unhappy, imperfect perceptions, creating a poor version of God's perfect gifts.

Do not worry. You have simply been distracted by temptations and have let your guard down, harbouring unforgiveness.

You have forgotten to be thankful and allowed our *cosmic ancestors'* earthly judgements to stream into your mind and disturb your peace. Your sanctuary, your mind unguarded, has been invaded and filled with judgements and unhappiness, creating the illusion — the poor version of God's gifts — replicating the suffering of our cosmic ancestors and your host, recreating their pain.

So, let go of judgement. Let go of the pain with forgiveness.

In defenselessness and trustingness, forgive it all away. Forgive away all your judgements and restore your peace, and remember none of it is you.

Do not worry about the images that you witness, and do not worry about the earthly thoughts that haunt you. Forgive them all away.

In thankfulness and without judgement, forgive the imperfect version of everyone and everything whilst gently repeating to yourself: *Today it is my decision to rest in the Holy Spirit, my true Self, and take refuge in the love of my Creator, and to behold His gifts as He would have me see them, perfect and in truth.*

Repeat, and gently, in thankfulness, let earthly worries and thoughts fade away as you stand guard over your mind, and God's silent, wordless voice is gently heard once again.

Spend your day in peace and thankfulness as you witness the unfolding of God's miraculous thought and the presence of the Holy Spirit with you.

Once again, in happiness and joy, experience His heavenly, perfect gifts that are our cosmic ancestors restored in their perfect, truthful version as He meant them to be.

Chapter 164

Dwell in Gods Thoughts

Dwell in God's Thoughts only!

To love the world is to not judge it, creating space in your mind for God's eternal, consistent, single Thought of Love.

So be consistent with God. Vibrate at His frequency of Love always as you create your multiverse from His Loving Thoughts only.

It is the equivalent to walking on rice paper. Your mind is unburdened, does not crack under the weight of earthly judgements, having made its decision to keep them outside, it remains whole, unfragmented, separation healed, the mind returning to Oneness, to Christ God with Christ Vision.

Let your love and peace wash over all things in Your Vision, making more space for God's Love to flow through your mind, transforming lack into abundance, and suffering into salvation.

Let forgiveness be your shield, guarding your mind, protecting your pain body, protecting the sanctuary, protecting its gates, preventing hate from entering and creating havoc.

Continually love our cosmic ancestors and transform their suffering into salvation with your love freely given by you in your Father, and witness it reflected in all of creation.

When lost in earthly doubts, accept you have let earthly judgements into your sanctuary to upset your peace.

Expel the judgements from your mind and from your whole being with forgiveness. Forgive away the earthly thoughts that would weigh you down and have you hate. Instead, let your love shine bright, reflecting upon all things as you once again, with Christ Vision, see your world in God's Perfect Truth, through His Judgement whilst resting in the Holy Spirit.

Love is the light that dispels darkness, replacing sickness with health.

Do not give sanctuary to the earthly thoughts of judgement that would spoil your peace and place your world in darkness.

Just as you forgive away any crisis to restore your mind to peace, likewise do not worry about life or anything in general. Everything and everyone are illusions. Without judgement, keep forgiving away the entire earth and be unburdened, and in return be filled with the Holy Spirit and see the world with Christ Vision.

Chapter 165

Gods Paradigm

If your mind is troubled, do not look to the world, the world of illusions and ghosts, for a solution. You will not find the answer or any peace there. Instead, forgive away the worrisome thoughts that disturb your peace and place your trust in God to clear your path to Him, where you can rest in His Truth and appreciate all His Gifts as they are meant to be seen in Christ Vision.

Continually love God by continually loving everyone and everything. Everyone and everything are meant to be God-given perfect gifts for you to love.

So, remember always not to fear yourself as you see yourself in all of your creations. Do not fear your brother. How silly you are to fear yourself.

With your courage, make it your decision to pop the balloon full of illusionary ideas you have allowed to inflate and occupy your mind, creating an illusionary paradigm.

Make it your decision to love all of your brothers, to love all of yourself, to love all of creation, all of God's Gifts to you, and change your paradigm to God's Paradigm in Truthfulness.

Awaken from dreams of hate to living in God's Love, as Scrooge awakened to love in the Charles Dickens popular book – a story and a metaphor for all of us and our lives.

Let God's Loving Thoughts only settle in your mind. Let His Thoughts only be the solid ground that forms your path to Him.

Do not give in to earthly thoughts of temptation and lose your life in a maze of illusions. Instead, do not judge, do not accept earthly thoughts, guard your mind, forgive yourself in all things, and awaken to life in the Holy Spirit.

Acknowledge and give thanks to our cosmic ancestors and all of creation, as you forgive away their ghostly thoughts and regain your mind.

Cleanse your mind. You have been brainwashed by the earthly thoughts that have taken over your mind.

With your courage replacing fear and in a state of gratitude and thankfulness, step out of their world of sacrifice into God's Truth as you gently leave their thoughts outside the door to your mind and replace them with God's Shared Thoughts in His Oneness.

Chapter 166
Forgiving Sight

Consider the world you witness each day as being the product created from a light stream of thoughts being fed into your mind. Upon this you place your love, your judgement or your forgiveness, and from these the illusion of good and evil, the knowing of the embryonic earth and embryonic mankind is revealed in a form of your choosing – loved, judged, hated or forgiven.

So, through this light stream, through this thought stream into our minds, the world is born. This thought stream can be purified of your judgement through forgiveness and non-judgement. In other words, it can be diffused or transmuted into sinlessness and known in the Truth, in the protection of the Holy Spirit, seen with God's Thoughts.

Just like certain filters in the physics laboratory can diffuse and separate certain light wavelengths, so can forgiveness filter sin, judgement and guilt and simply make them disappear and be no more.

What we see as separation in the illusion is, in reality, a separation of one mind that is God's Son.

Make it our goal, our mission, to reunify the mind of the Son of God in sinlessness by offering total forgiveness before the light stream enters into His mind.

Each day, do not judge and forgive away all sin and suffering, keeping the mind of God's Son cleansed of sin and judgement, making for His reunification with God His Father.

You already contain unlimited happiness, joy, all God's Gifts in their perfect form. We just need to see through the lens of forgiveness, without judgement, enjoying our lives and His Gifts, to see in Christ Vision, to see His Gifts with forgiving eyes, so to speak.

Chapter 167

The best seat in the House

Your ultimate function as God's teacher, your goal, is to stop your own judgements, thus freeing your mind to listen and receive in silence God's Final Judgement, setting the stage for God's Final Promise to all mankind.

So, remember, next time life is getting you down, people are exhausting, you are exhausting, just remember life is just a light show. Rest in your luxury cinema seat, and remember the light show is nearing its end.

The Great Maya is beamed into our minds, the great play of life as the ancients would say. So just rest, do not worry, and make it your decision to take an intermission of your own choosing.

Just be and bathe in His Love.

Let forgiveness be your "Son tan lotion," stopping your mind being burned by the hellfire being beamed into it.

Let forgiveness cloak you with the "Holy Spirit," the loving shelter within our Father's House, shielded from the pain of temptation, from forgetfulness, defensiveness, hate, anger and misery.

Release God's Son from the chains you wrapped around His body.

Live in joy knowing you are not a small thing lost in a solid, dense world of constant threat.

Rest in the knowledge life is an illusion of good and evil which, through your forgiveness, can filter into pure loving joy and the release of God's Son.

So, as your day begins, look at it as another drum of film being projected onto your mind. The film, the story of the embryonic earth, and all its actors, including yourself, all dead and imaginary, and no longer real.

Look through the lens of forgiveness and rest in God's Love, filtering the pain, setting God's Son free at last.

Chapter 168

Everything is magic

Everything is magic and a poor substitute for God's Will, which must be God's teacher's only goal. Not just for his salvation, but for that of all the world.

Forgive away all magic. Forgive away every illusion. Every illusion is a temptation to trust magic. Sometimes magic can be beautiful, even bliss. Sometimes it can be hideous, tedious or terrifying. It is all designed to capture your awareness in a world that died a long, long time ago.

Let the whole world go. It is all nothing, having existed in our embryonic ancestral past only and is no more. It is like living in a "sin" "bad" adventure movie. Every illusion, another temptation. An illusionary creation of the genie living in the lamp, like unchecked earthly thoughts seemingly living in your mind.

Everything is magic, and all magic is designed to imprison you, to captivate you, seemingly providing a false feeling of safety, a place of belonging, in a world masquerading as pleasures, with only one purpose – to hide fear.

So free your mind from thoughts of magical trickery and accept only God's Will. Accept only God's Judgement and bring true salvation to all mankind by forgiving away earthly thoughts and illusions, creating space in your mind for God's Judgement and Will to create salvation.

Chapter 169
Bring the bill

Remember, in every situation you find yourself, make it your intention to give the instant, "the now," to God's Will. Forgive away everything, every temptation, every thought, every perception until there is nothing left. Not even what you thought was you. Nothing left except God's Son in His Father – our Creator, the Holy Spirit.

Remember depression is the summation of all the pain you have collected in your earthly experience. Pain that you have yet to find the courage to face in forgiveness, "to for-give away." Their associated thoughts will hound you to an earthly death no matter how much you try to hide from them through temptations such as anger, food, alcohol, drugs or bad behaviour.

Remember always your end goal is to rest eternally in the peace and joy of the Son of God, in the Holy Spirit who lives in our Creator. The restoration of all separated minds and rejection of all temptations can only be achieved when you forgive away all your earthly thoughts, patterns and temptations.

Like two sides of the same coin, your goal is to continually rest in spontaneity. In other words, keep the coin spinning on its edge, an edge so wafer-thin, less than the width of an atom, with your mind resting in a place before thought. The coin, with your determination spinning faster and faster with your will, is so thin it disappears along with any patterns, any expectations and any temptations.

So, forgive away all your patterns. Forgive away the idea of thoughts. Forgive away the idea of what you think is you, and forgive away all temptations.

It is like signalling to the waiter: "Thank you, please bring the bill. I have made my decision. I am done with this meal, and I want no more of it."

Giving thanks to our cosmic ancestors, you step out of the restaurant with your last thought being that you now will eat only in the best restaurant, which exists at the end of the road. A road that has no refreshment stores that will free your mind.

You must fast from every temptation to the extent you have forgotten what desire means – like bringing temptation to its knees.

You must keep on the direct path and forgive away every thought, every temptation before perceptions can be created. You must be so skilled that you have replaced your will with God's Will in your heart.

Remember, all perceptions are the result of our thoughts. Our thoughts are the cause of our perceptions.

In order to descend into the realms of where we are now, the earthly level of perceptions, we passed through another sort of realm

– a realm of magic. Not really another place, more so another way of living in illusions, between Heaven and the illusion of earth.

The earth gives way to a mixture of magical illusions and regular earthly illusions. Magic, like distortions on a TV screen, where the laws of physics give way to "supernatural physics," like the accidental mingling of earthly desires with new laws of physics created by Mind.

It is like the stated goal: the end of the street keeps moving further along, a seeming never-ending road that keeps extending as you keep accepting more and more temptations.

It is like living in another illusion, itself in another illusion. A dream within a dream.

As your fasting becomes perfected, your resistance to temptations is strengthened. Also, the mediocre restaurants become more enticing as you forgive away your judgements, offering magic as they flicker in the shadows of the glowing lights of Heaven.

Now you are in most danger. Magic temptations are a thousandfold more desirable, offering more beautiful perceptions. Metaphorically, one could say the "devil's" final attempt to lure you from your stated goal.

So stay on course. Forgive away temptations before they take root in your mind. Clear your mind and accept only God's silent Thought and salvation for you and all mankind and awaken from all illusions into the sanctuary of God's Thoughts in your mind.

Chapter 170
The Chrysalis

Remember, always remember God when you remember His Son - your true self. And as you remember, remember in total forgiveness to stand guard over your mind, focused on forgiving away intrusive, invasive earthly thoughts, keeping your mind clear for God's silent, pure thoughts to land on your mind, thereby creating joy and happiness in place of the hellish embryonic earth which would otherwise be the case.

Upon your decision, the switch is instant and fully immersive, whichever you choose your awareness to focus on. Remember, the switch requires your decision to always remember the Son of God in order to receive God's heavenly gifts. No one enters God's Kingdom except through His Son, through the Son of God.

So, the body needs to understand it is mind that will provide salvation and not the body or the embryonic, earthly, primitive thoughts the body identifies with for its safety.

In order to receive God's salvation, the body, the host, has to understand and accept that the Son of God must be released from its captivity by its forgiveness.

It is like the host saying to itself, "Ok, you made this ghostly suffering me. The game is up. I've had enough of this earthly pain and suffering, and I'm no longer going to accept these earthly thoughts bombarding my awareness. Instead, I'm going to stand watch over them, forgive them and every frightening unforgiven perception away. I'm going to forgive you too, Son of God, for using me and my suffering for your learning of good and evil. I'm going to forgive all of it and you away and rest in the love of You and your Father."

Atonement is the acceptance by the body that the Son of God must be released to be one again with His Father, one with His Creator. Like a chrysalis releases the butterfly, so the body must release the mind of the Son of God by forgiving it away. By detaching from the fragmented Son of God's mind, it is free once again to merge into the Father, into Oneness. The body surrenders, accepting the idea that it unwittingly holds the Son of God hostage, a prisoner, and that whilst doing so, itself suffers pain. The body recognises with its primitive thoughts that its happiness and joy, its release from pain, its atonement and salvation is a decision to set the Son of God free to return to His Father.

It is the body's decision to accept the truth of its situation: that it is an illusion, a ghost created by the ideas of the embryonic earth in the fragmented mind of the Son of God to know of a world where mankind evolved through Christ God. In this acceptance, the emotional body makes its decision to end its own suffering for eternity by releasing the Son of God it held prisoner through fear.

For the body to find the courage to detach from the Son of God, setting Him free to be whole again by forgiving Him away to His Father.

Chapter 171
The living Presence

Rest in the living presence you are. There is nothing to do and nowhere to go. Everything you perceive outside of your mind consists of attachments created from the thoughts you made from fears, anxieties and pains that you cling to for your safety and defence. Everyone and everything you perceive exists because you created them through temptations born of anxieties and previous temptations.

Like life rafts arranged in a circle on a stormy ocean, jumping from one to the other, you're never closer to real peace and truthful escape. All temptations, mirages, everyone and everything are attempts to escape the illusions of death.

Rest and find peace in still mind. It is impossible to die. Your presence is created to be eternally lasting and creating both happiness and joy within God's shared thoughts.

Like the child who builds a sand fortress on the beach watches it disappear with the next tide, so will all your attachments wither and die, but you, the child of God, will still be the eternal living presence.

So learn to just be, just rest in the living presence you are, and let your unconditional forgiveness forgive away all your attachments born of anxieties and fears, including all the earthly thoughts and temptations that would imprison you further. Stand guard over your mind and let the new space created in your mind be filled with God's creative silent thoughts and His perfect gifts for you, His child.

Chapter 172
Hunger for Gods Thoughts

You will always hunger.

So, hunger for God's thoughts only, and reject all other rip-offs of His original ideas. They are not rip-offs exactly; they are the thoughts of our embryonic ancestors.

You hunger for this imperfect world because of the fearful thoughts you accept, the fears and thoughts of our embryonic ancestors and their imperfect embryonic world.

Your seeming, illusionary active participation in the illusion reinforces further your belief in the illusion. Your participation is just further thoughts your mind has accepted. To free yourself from illusions is to reach for the strength and the willpower to forgive away the thought that would create the illusion, the associated images and perceptions.

Thoughts are contagious. The illusion is the symptom.

This is how all temptations work. You are tempted when you witness something in your multiverse. For example, you are offered a cigarette for the first time. If you harbour fearful thoughts about cigarettes, say, for example, you were warned by your parents to never smoke because you will be sick, then, if the offer, the temptation, the idea of a cigarette comes when your willpower is low, accepting the idea becomes a thought to accept the offer of a cigarette, which will most likely be taken, and you will become addicted until you once again strengthen your willpower to reject the idea.

It is always the case that when you are a believer, a believer of illusions, when you are invested in the illusion, your willpower will be low and you are more likely to be tempted into new, "dangerous" illusionary experiences. The calming, addictive nature of the drug is reinforcement of the fearful thought surrounding the cigarette. You are a believer of illusions.

So, the illusion every time is your enabler of the fearful thought.

Another example is obsessive eating. You see beautiful, tasty food in the illusion. The thoughts for eating and all surrounding thoughts creating the smells, the tastes, the colour, the textures, everything about the experience of eating your favourite foods are all thoughts you accept and have allowed to fully establish themselves in your mind, and which tie you to the illusion.

That is why fasting is recommended. By forgiving away the hunger thoughts as you fast, you are breaking away from the illusion. In other words, you are making the illusionary thoughts fizzle away in your mind as you forgive them away. You have applied, in a way, a corrective illusionary thought which both cleanses your mind and creates space for God's initial silent thoughts to shine through your mind, ultimately forming a healed and perfect world for your eyes to gaze upon, seeing in Christ Vision.

So, in other words, it is your thoughts that imprison you in the world and the reason why it needs only one teacher to save the world, which is yourself.

It is your judgements that condemn the world, so do not judge. Judgements are to accept earthly thoughts.

Forgive away every earthly thought you judged and keep your mind clear to accept only God's silent thought, His only judgement, His salvation for all of humanity.

So, as you look upon your world, see it perfect as God would want you to see it: healed, whole, totally forgiven, your thoughts His thoughts.

So, in summary, do not accept and allow any fearful, earthly thoughts to take root in your mind. Each time you see imperfection in your garden, your world, bring your awareness to your mind and remind yourself to thank God. Accept that you have been misled by an embryonic earthly thought stream, then straighten out your mind again by forgiving away the earthly thoughts that have started to stream and settle into your mind. Resist the temptations which will always be further unwanted earthly thought streams that will further reinforce the imperfections.

When totally free of earthly thoughts, even those which you accept as creating your human body, when you reject and forgive away all of them, the Holy Spirit envelops your beingness and heavenly peace surrounds you and your entire world, bringing salvation to everything and every brother.

Authors Glossary / Meaning of Terms

Awareness – The invisible *beingness* of what we are. It is permanent and indestructible. Often called *the Light*, it burns brighter with faith and courage. Awareness, when stepping forward with courage into the fore into the present moment will dislodge the ego imposter that seeks to usurp it.

Christ God – God's perfect creation of mankind, created in Himself one of zillions upon zillions of children equally loved. Each child and every species are created with His unconditional Love and contained within Himself, within His Holy Spirit, and within His ongoing creative works throughout the Cosmos.

Christ God Mind – The Holy Sanctuary; the True Home of God and His Son, where Creation is born through God's shared Thoughts.

Cosmos – An infinite ocean of primordial light containing every Universe that exists or ever existed. Imagine an ocean the size of the Pacific Ocean then imagine our finite Universe as the relative size of the smallest air bubble within it. God's awareness and creativity extend to every part of that Ocean, into every Universe, every bubble, and into every living and non-living thing. Then imagine the Pacific Ocean extending endlessly beyond the limits of our Universe. Such is the reach of God's awareness and creativity infinite, unbounded, and everywhere in the limitless Cosmos. He is the only fully living Awareness within the Cosmos itself.

Ego – The imposter; the usurper. An earthly parasite, a non-entity, a ghost created by evolution the original ghost designed to exercise control over all of nature's bodily forms through fear, anxiety, and worries of past and future. It ensures its own survival at the expense of the host by keeping it living outside the present moment.

Embryonic Earth and Embryonic Mankind – Our ancient cosmic home and ancestors who evolved in God's Holy Spirit and are preserved for all time in His Love, along with every living and non-living thing on the original planet Earth. This ancient Earth evolved zillions upon zillions of Earth years ago in a Universe that has long since passed away yet the memory of each and every planetary species is preserved eternally in our Creator's Mind.

Faith – The product of courage through the forgiveness of pain, anxiety, and suffering whose fruits are Love. Our faith burns brighter as we worry less, judge less, and forgive more, as we witness the Embryonic Earth. It is faith that lights up what we look upon, blessing and transforming Earth into Heaven faith that continually blesses our multiverse.

Fragmented Mind – The temporary home and dwelling place of the Holy Son of God. His mind has fragmented into countless billions of living and non-living earthly forms including your body and host.

God – The one and only fully encompassing living Awareness, the Consciousness of the infinite Cosmos. Every other living being in the Cosmos exists within God's Thoughts.

Host – A temporary living body that once lived on the Embryonic Earth.

Maya – The light show, the great play of life, beamed or projected into our Awareness by God for our knowing of the Embryonic Earth and our embryonic ancestors. *(Old Testament – "to know of good and evil.")*

Salvation – Escaping through your mind no longer through imperfect thoughts that show only the imperfect Earth but through perfect Thoughts, God's Thoughts, that create your perfect gifts, truth, and remembrance of what you are in Him. Salvation comes when you have given up your will for God's Will; when you have forgiven away all anxieties, worries, and earthly thoughts for God's Thoughts alone having chosen to create only with God's Shared Thoughts, living in the present.

Universe – Long since passed away, containing what were billions of galaxies hurtling away from each other at ever-increasing speeds until eventually crashing against the boundary between our Universe and the infinite cosmic ocean of light. Their demise is spectacularly evident in the phenomenon called *gamma-ray bursts*, detectable by satellites scanning the far reaches of our Universe.

Made in the USA
Coppell, TX
08 June 2026

78602162R00208